Advance praise for *This Band of Sisterhood*

"There are so many nugget   .1-
versations between these rei   ...iiops that
when you have finished the t   .. need to read it again
for a second, third, and fourth time! The reflections, experiences,
and profound humanity that my sisters share in these pages are
indeed priceless."

—THE MOST REV. MICHAEL B. CURRY
Presiding Bishop of The Episcopal Church

"*This Band of Sisterhood* is personal, spiritual, theological, and
political. With each conversation, it becomes clear that these
five Black women bishops are not content with being 'first'
and that they refuse to be essentialized as symbols of diversity. Instead, they are determined to carry forth the legacy of
the Rt. Rev. Barbara Harris, Pauli Murray, and the other Black
women who dared the church to live into its call to be a witness
to God's just future in an unjust present. *This Band of Sisterhood* is a sign of hope that our church is indeed on the path to
becoming Church."

—THE VERY REV. KELLY BROWN DOUGLAS, PHD
Dean, Episcopal Divinity School
at Union Theological Seminary

"We are changed by the sacred stories of one another, especially
if the stories are of persons to which the world does not always
listen. *This Band of Sisterhood* is a precious offering, a divinely
crafted mosaic of devoted and tenacious faithfulness, a challenge

to the reader to pursue with greater clarity and vigor the Spirit's liberating work of justice in both church and world, and just good food for the soul!"

—THE RT. REV. MARY GRAY-REEVES
Managing Director, College for Bishops,
The Episcopal Church

"I am so excited to commend this book to you. These are our sisters, those elevated and now celebrated, as women paving the paths that were blazed for them. Did I say blaze? These bishops are on fire—a must-read."

—THE REV. DR. SUZAN JOHNSON COOK
Ambassador at Large for International Religious Freedom,
the Obama administration

THIS BAND OF
SISTERHOOD

Black Women Bishops

ON RACE, FAITH, AND THE CHURCH

Edited by
WESTINA MATTHEWS

Morehouse Publishing
NEW YORK

Morehouse Publishing, 19 East 34th Street, New York, NY 10016
Morehouse Publishing is an imprint of Church Publishing Incorporated.

Cover photo by Phillip MacVean. *From left to right:* The Rt. Rev. Kimberly (Kym) Lucas, the Rt. Rev. Jennifer Baskerville-Burrows, the Rt. Rev. Phoebe A. Roaf, the Rt. Rev. Carlye J. Hughes, the Rt. Rev. Dr. Shannon MacVean-Brown
Cover design by Marc Whitaker, MTWdesign
Interior design and typesetting by Beth Oberholtzer Design

Library of Congress Cataloging-in-Publication Data

Names: Matthews, Westina, 1948– editor.
Title: This band of sisterhood : Black women bishops on race, faith, and the church / edited by Westina Matthews.
Description: New York, NY : Church Publishing, [2021]
Identifiers: LCCN 2021005789 (print) | LCCN 2021005790 (ebook) | ISBN 9781640653511 (paperback) | ISBN 9781640653528 (epub)
Subjects: LCSH: African American women clergy. | Episcopal Church— Bishops.
Classification: LCC BX5967 .T45 2021 (print) | LCC BX5967 (ebook) | DDC 283.092/520973—dc23
LC record available at https://lccn.loc.gov/2021005789
LC ebook record available at https://lccn.loc.gov/2021005790

To the Rt. Rev. Barbara Clementine Harris
(June 12, 1930–March 13, 2020)
of blessed memory

CONTENTS

Foreword

... AND A BAND OF ANGELS

When you strike the women, you strike a rock

from the South African History Archive

I have added an ellipsis to the title of this piece because it seems fitting to me that the lovely book title *This Band of Sisterhood* could also include *and a band of angels* as a way to describe further the warrior women bishops highlighted in the pages to follow. This inspiring chronicle of their journeys helps us to see clearly how they embody the spirit of the beautiful words from the South African women declaring their stalwart strength.

"When you strike the women, you strike a rock" can be applied to some extent to women across the globe and the ages, but women of color and especially African American women have embodied the truth of that image in ways that set them apart from white women. (I have deliberately chosen to use "African American" rather than "Black," as for me a term that denotes a history separate from slavery is important.) There was no place called "ladyhood" reserved for them even when they displayed all of the characteristics of being ladies. The lack of respect meted out to persons left to live on the margins is phenomenal and African American women have been and continue to be invited to stay on the margins of mainstream American life, even in the Episcopal Church.

The election of six African American women as diocesan bishops in the past three years seems to offer a hopeful sign about the possibilities for the future. As I write, we are less than a month away from the amazing event of the inauguration of a South Asian/Jamaican woman as vice president of the United States. Both of these are events that African American foremothers would not have been able to imagine.

Sojourner Truth, Harriet Tubman, Ida B. Wells, and many others who spent their lives in the challenging struggle for freedom and the right to be seen as a worthy child of God would not have been able to imagine this day. If they had not taken the paths that they chose, however, this progress would have been impossible. All who are paying attention know that African American women stand on their shoulders.

The fierceness of Sojourner Truth in declaring, "Ain't I a woman?" rings through the hearts and ears of every African American woman who decides that the margin is not good enough for her. Highlights from the lives of two of these women are given in order to clearly reflect upon the warrior woman and sisterhood tradition that these bishops are helping to continue:

Fannie Lou Hamer learned many powerful lessons about what happens to the African American woman who decides that the margin is not good enough for her when she decided to fight for voting rights. She almost lost her life and did lose her sharecropper's shack after being expelled from the farm where she worked. In spite of that, however, she continued to persevere in her fight to be represented by her state, Mississippi, as a worthy human being who did not have to settle for living on the margin. Fannie Lou Hamer is a profound example of striking a rock.

Ida B. Wells understood that she did not have maleness, ladyhood, or whiteness to provide support for her and that she had to work for her freedom as well as other African Americans. She was clear about her call. She has a stellar historical record of "turning on the light of truth" on evils and wrongdoing from the time that she was sixteen years old until she passed away in 1931, refusing to be silenced and made invisible. She stood against the racism of white women in the quest for gender equality as they attempted to force her to be invisible so that their racism could prevail. She refused to cooperate with them in that regard. Along with her bold work for women's rights was the phenomenal work that she did in fighting against lynching. She made it clear that lynching was yet another facet of the overall systemic racism and hatred for Black bodies that existed.

Wells was highly respected for the fierceness that she brought to the discussion on lynching. Even Frederick Douglass confessed that she enlightened him about the ways in which the lynched had their character lynched as well as their bodies. He along with white people began to realize that racism provided the foundation for lynching. Wells was a careful documenter of the facts around numerous lynchings and uncompromising in her analysis and this caused her newspaper office to be burned and a bounty placed upon her for years.

Bishop Barbara C. Harris must be acknowledged for her willingness to stand for election as the first African American woman bishop in the Episcopal Church amidst the threats of violence and expressions of disdain by her male clergy colleagues. She demonstrated extraordinary courage and ability to hold to the difficult path as she navigated her way forward. Her uncompromising faith in God and herself and the best sense of humor to be found on the earth helped her to weather the storms she lived through while blazing this trail. All African American women who follow her need to remember her contribution.

The angelic band of sisters and foremothers include so many women; unfortunately, we will never know the names of many of them. What we do know is that without their willingness to hold to the difficult liberation journey, African American women would not be thriving as they are in 2021. The Episcopal Church has elected six amazing women diocesan bishops who are continuing that long legacy of resistance. Their stories, contained in this book, about their respective paths to this point inspires, brings the reader to tears, and makes the reader wish to stand a bit taller and to be a bit more courageous.

Their stories show us their humanity as well as their fierce and uncompromising pursuit of life as they want it to be. It is important to pay attention to their humanity. Just as Fannie Lou, Ida B., Sojourner, Harriett, Mary McLeod, Bishop Barbara, and all of the others before them and all who are to come must be seen as women above all other designations. African American women have spent far too much energy and time proving their humanity, deserving of the life that they wish to have. Wells fought hard to make sure that African Americans were seen as human beings and not some extraordinary species. The need to relegate African Americans to super human or nonhuman status is simply another facet of a racist ideology that refuses to accept African Americans as equals.

The dioceses that have been smart enough to elect this "band of angelic sisters" would do well to allow them to be human beings first, bishops second, and then African American women. The process of accepting them and their power will be one of the greatest challenges that each of these dioceses face. It continues to be easier for whites to romanticize racial equality than to live into the reality of it. The call to the Episcopal Church in this present moment is to stand taller and listen more carefully to the call to be who God wants it to be. God did not create the racial divide; human beings made those divisions and God is not pleased with them. The soul of the human person requires freedom. The Church's most important task is sharing the message that freedom is necessary and the way to find it. Therefore, it cannot be true to that message of providing a pathway to true freedom while participating in oppressing.

This "band of bishops" will bring their gifts, keen minds, great spirits, leadership skills, vision, passion, histories, wounds, and ways of being in the world to their respective episcopacies; they will not bring "maleness, whiteness, and the ways we have always done it" to their work if they are true to God's call to them. The Church will never be what God wishes it to be until all its members are willing to accept that it is made up of a diverse group of folks, all loved equally by the God who made them and who rules the universe. The Church needs to remember the message from Peter's dream of the basket with all kinds of animals, those familiar and those he did not recognize, and the invitation given to him to select from it for his meal. He realized that the dream was about the kingdom and accepting all of creation because God does not make unclean and unfit humans.

"When you strike the women, you strike a rock," and let the Church say, "Amen." Yes, the Church knows that "more change is going to come" and this band of angelic sister bishops are the best testimony to the hope and courage that will help to bring the change and that has undergirded this rock solid warrior women tradition for centuries. Carry on, Sister Bishops.

CATHERINE MEEKS
Absalom Jones Center for Racial Healing

INTRODUCTION

The idea for this book began with a happenstance conversation with the Rt. Rev. Phoebe A. Roaf on a Sunday in August 2019 at the airport in Colorado Springs, Colorado, as we awaited ground transportation to carry us to a Gathering of Leaders[1] meeting. Bishop Phoebe was exploring the possibility of joining the board and I was there as a facilitator for one of the organization's quarterly gatherings. As we stood outside, searching for the van, the bishop shared with me how the Black women clergy in the Episcopal Church had voiced a need to come together with the five Black women serving as diocesan bishops. The Black women clergy believed that their needs, experiences, and concerns were very different from Black male clergy and would welcome an opportunity to meet with the five bishops for an open, candid conversation.

With the #MeToo movement top of mind for many of us and in light of the increasing division in our country, I knew that these five Black women bishops could provide a compass for how to navigate these new, unchartered pathways. This was an historical moment for the Episcopal Church and their story needed to be told and it needed to be heard. While I could not facilitate a meeting of the Black women clergy, perhaps I could edit a book based on conversations with the bishops.

There was only one problem. I did not feel that I was your "typical" Episcopalian. I was raised in the AME Church, coming from a long line of ministers—including my father, my uncle, and my grandfather. Further, I have only been an Episcopalian for about fifteen years, unlike some of my "cradle" Episcopalian friends. I jokingly tell everyone that I kept the "E" in the AME in my family. And yes, while I have been an adjunct professor at General Theological Seminary for ten years, I teach contemplative spiritual direction in the Center for Christian Spirituality. My doctorate and postdoctorate fellowships were in education, not theology. Still, my commitment to the development and advancement of women and people of color—especially in leadership positions—spans over forty years as an educational researcher, a grantmaker, a public servant, and an author.

I had never even met the four other Black women bishops; and only Bishop Phoebe for about fifteen minutes standing in front of an airport. In spite of my own reservations, I felt Spirit-led to pursue this idea for a book, and things began to move quickly. With her enthusiastic support, Bishop Phoebe was my initial liaison with the other bishops to determine if there was interest. Holding my prayer breath, I awaited their answer. They all agreed to participate. This was an answered prayer.

The legacy of Black women bishops begins with the Rt. Rev. Barbara C. Harris, who on September 24, 1988, was elected suffragan bishop (that is, a bishop who assists another bishop but does not have rights to succession) of the Episcopal Diocese of Massachusetts. She was consecrated on February 11, 1989, becoming the first woman to be ordained and consecrated a bishop in the worldwide Anglican Communion. It was only fifteen years prior that the Episcopal Church had first ordained women as priests. Upon retiring from her position in 2003,

Bishop Harris was succeeded as bishop suffragan by another Black woman, the Rt. Rev. Gayle Elizabeth Harris. This was the first time in the Episcopal Church in the United States that a woman was succeeded as bishop by another woman.

It was not until thirteen years later when, on October 28, 2016, the Rt. Rev. Jennifer Baskerville-Burrows was elected the 11th bishop of the Episcopal Diocese of Indianapolis (consecrated on April 29, 2017) that a Black woman was elected a diocesan bishop in the denomination's 185-year history. Succeeding the Rt. Rev. Catherine Elizabeth Maples Waynick, Bishop Jennifer was also the first woman to succeed another woman as diocesan bishop.[2]

In three very short years, following Bishop Baskerville-Burrows's election, there were now a total of *five* Black women serving as diocesan bishops:

The Rt. Rev. Carlye J. Hughes was consecrated on September 22, 2018, as the 11th bishop of Newark, becoming the first woman and first Black elected bishop in Newark in its 145-year history.

The Rt. Rev. Phoebe A. Roaf was consecrated as the fourth bishop of the Diocese of West Tennessee on May 4, 2019, becoming both the first woman and the first Black bishop in the diocese's 36-year history.

The Rt. Rev. Kimberly (Kym) Lucas was consecrated on May 18, 2019, as the 11th bishop of the Diocese of Colorado, becoming the first woman bishop as well as the first Black bishop in the diocese's 132-year history.

The Rt. Rev. Dr. Shannon MacVean-Brown was consecrated as the 11th bishop of the Diocese of Vermont on September 28, 2019, becoming the first Black and the first Black woman bishop in the diocese's 229-year history. Bishop Shannon also is one of only three Black women (following Rt. Rev. Barbara Harris and the Rt. Rev. Gayle Harris) to hold the title of bishop in any of the seven dioceses that make up the Episcopal Church in New England, also known as Province I of the Episcopal Church.

At the time this book was conceived, women numbered only twenty-seven, or 20.6 percent, of the total 131 active bishops (diocesan, suffragan, assistant, or assisting), including all those elected but yet to be ordained.[3] Therefore, these five Black women bishops represented only 4 percent of the 131 active diocesan bishops. With such an important role in the Episcopal Church, I believed that these amazing women had much to offer ecclesiastically, spiritually, and practically.

In November 2019, when I first proposed this book to Church Publishing Incorporated, I could never imagine what 2020 would hold: a pandemic, racial unrest, and a highly charged presidential election. Our original plan was to begin our conversations just before the Episcopal Church House of Bishops meeting began in March 2020 at Camp Allen in Texas, with three video conference meetings to follow. With COVID-19 quickly becoming a reality, the House of Bishops meeting would now be held virtually, and our meeting was cancelled.

The timeline for this book became questionable. Our shared grief and disbelief of the murder of Ahmaud Arbery—a twenty-five-year old Black man who was murdered on February 23, 2020, by armed white men as he was jogging in Glynn County, Georgia—took our breaths away. With all of the unanticipated delays, COVID-19, and the racial unrest, I began to wonder if this book could become a reality.

Nevertheless, the project moved forward. I invited Catherine Meeks, PhD, executive director of the Absalom Jones Center for Racial Healing, to write a foreword. I continued to hold each of the bishops in prayer, following them on social media, and receiving encouragement and strength through their Harriett Tubman–like efforts to free others from fear, anxiety, loneliness, and grief.

Our first virtual meeting was scheduled for March 17, and the month was filled with unexpected events. On March 4, Bishop Phoebe spoke at a Lenten Lecture program at St. Paul's Episcopal Church in Chattanooga, Tennessee, and nine days later the Rev. Brad Whittaker, the rector of that parish, was diagnosed with COVID-19. Tennessee had declared a "state of emergency" on March 12, and Bishop Roaf was in self-quarantine.

Bishop Barbara Harris died on March 13, 2020, at the age of eighty-nine. She was a mentor to and source of inspiration for these five Black women bishops, and their grief was palpable. The agenda for this brief meeting was to see if the book was even a viable option and, if so, to identify potential topics. I immediately became aware how glad they were to see one another on the computer screen, as they shared their own grappling with circumstances and responsibilities. Yes, they still wanted to go forward with the book. However, they asked if we could wait awhile before beginning the conversations.

We did not meet again until June 3. Over the next five months, we met five times, and it became clear that this book was even more important than I originally had envisioned. These prayer warrior women had much to share, against the backdrop of the pandemic, the racial unrest and protests, and the presidential election. Indeed, I thought I had all the material that I needed after our virtual meeting in October, but the aftermath of the presidential election persuaded me that another meeting was needed. Blessedly, the five bishops all agreed without hesitation.

The following chapters are presented in the sequence of our virtual meetings. However, to facilitate the reader's accessibility to the conversations, there are a few times that I have reserved particular discussions to other chapters. I learned early on that while I could pose questions for each of the sessions, their responses rarely would directly answer the questions but rather serve as a springboard to begin a conversation among themselves. To provide a context for what was happening in the country at the time of the virtual meeting, I have begun each chapter by setting the contextual scene.

Each of the six meetings was recorded and transcribed. I have tried to remain true to their voices with only a light editing of their words, using brackets sparingly for clarification. To ease understanding of who was speaking, the bishops gracefully gave me permission to refer to them as "Bishop" with their first name.

As we journeyed together over the months, I witnessed a band of sisterhood being formed. Having promised to honor their occasional requests to "don't put this in the book," I am humbled by the privilege to be able to listen in on their conversations.

At the end of each of our conversations, I would invite one of the bishops to offer a prayer. Heartfelt and spontaneous, I knew that each of the chapters would conclude with one of their prayers.

Just as I was finishing up the manuscript for the book, the Rev. Canon Paula E. Clark, canon to the ordinary and chief of staff, Diocese of Washington, was elected on December 12, 2020, to be the 13th bishop of the Diocese of Chicago, becoming the first Black person and first woman to hold this position in the diocese; she was scheduled to be consecrated on April 24, 2021. Bishop Paula graciously agreed to contribute an afterword for this book.

The title for the book is inspired by the prayer offered by Bishop Carlye. Yes, this band of sisterhood—which began thirty-one years ago with Bishop Barbara Harris and continues today with these now six Black women bishops—is a mighty bond shared among women who "completely get it."

Dear Heavenly Father, we come before you, completely trusting in your goodness and mercy. I appeal to your loving spirit to watch over these women gathered for this book. I praise you for their lives and their souls and I am filled with deep gratitude. Look upon my sisters with your tenderness and grace. Bless these women. Let them be healthy, free, and protected in the strength of your loving arms. In these things I pray, Amen.

WESTINA MATTHEWS
Week of Advent IV, 2020

Chapter 1

GIRD UP MY LOINS

Setting the Scene

Our second meeting was not held until June 3, 2020. Almost three months had passed since our initial virtual meeting on March 17, and COVID-19 was taking its toll. The U.S. Centers for Disease Control and Prevention reported 1.76 million total cases (23,553 new) and 103,700 deaths (915 new). While the total of COVID-19 deaths was continuing to decline, the total number of deaths still had surpassed 100,000.[1]

The hurricane season also had begun. But most pressing on the minds of these women and for most Black people was the increased racial unrest, protesting the historically unrelenting injustices against Blacks, or as Bishop Phoebe so eloquently stated in her letter to the diocese of June 2:

> I have not witnessed this level of collective anger and grief during my lifetime. I have deliberately been silent because there are no words to express how I feel in the depths of my soul. Over the past week, I have experienced anger, shock, fear, grief, and a profound sadness. All of these emotions are still present.[2]

It began with the murder of unarmed Black man Ahmaud Arbery, who was fatally shot by two white men after being chased while jogging on February 23. On May 5, a video of the murder was posted on a local radio station website in Brunswick, Georgia, for the world to see.

Breonna Taylor, a Black medical worker, had been killed by a white plainclothes police officer who entered her home in Louisville, Kentucky, on March 13. This case was drawing national attention in protests.

On May 25, Christian Cooper, a Black man who was an avid birder, was confronted by a white woman in Central Park, New York City. She had called the police to report that a Black man was threatening her. Fortunately, Cooper had recorded the entire incident on his phone and the video had gone viral.

Also, on May 25, police officers had arrested George Floyd, a Black man, in Minneapolis, Minnesota, and the following day the video of a police officer's knee on Mr. Floyd's neck for eight minutes and forty-six seconds was viewed around the world. His funeral was to be held on the day after our virtual meeting.

And on June 1, two days before the next scheduled meeting with the five bishops, then President Donald Trump stood in front of St. John's Episcopal Church in Lafayette Square, after peaceful protestors had been dispersed by the National Guard. On the morning of our meeting, Bishop Mariann Edgar Budde of the Episcopal Diocese of Washington was interviewed by NPR's Morning Edition, stating: "I am outraged."[3]

On June 2, Bishop Shannon issued a public letter, Reaffirming Our Renunciation of Evil, in part stating:

> The circumstances of the pandemic and the current unrest have brought this nation to a place where we can no longer

deny the brokenness of a society that is built on the subjugation and oppression of many while a few control most of the economic wealth. The church must call out this systemic callousness and disregard for the dignity of human beings. We must realize that striving for peace will make us uncomfortable and challenge many to give up their privilege.[4]

Bishop Carlye also had a pastoral letter to the Diocese of Newark entitled "What Direction Shall We Choose as Health Crisis and Racism Intersect with Faith and Politics?":

We had yet to get our bearings on the journey through the pandemic when the violent slayings of Ahmaud Arbery and George Floyd thrust us suddenly on to a treacherous but familiar side road. The dangers of COVID-19 have not diminished. It has become even more clear in the last twelve weeks that Blacks have a particular susceptibility to the virus. Theories abound about poverty and preexisting conditions, but these theories do nothing to explain the death of young, healthy, professional Blacks. Could it be that the wear and tear of navigating racism adversely impacts the resiliency of Blacks?[5]

Also, on June 2, The Episcopal Church's Department of Reconciliation, Justice and Creation Care and the Office of Government Relations, as a response to racist violence, made available resources to assist individuals, congregations, and communities.[6]

Just before it was time for us to meet on June 3, three of the Minnesota police officers had charges elevated to aiding and abetting murder; and the murder charge against the police officer whose knee was on the neck of George Floyd was elevated from third to second degree. It was the ninth day of protests across the country with curfews in place in many of the larger cities. The televised funeral for George Floyd was scheduled for the following day and the Rev. Al Sharpton would be giving the eulogy.

The Conversation Begins

The bishops immediately expressed their eagerness to spend this time together. I quickly realized that I had under-appreciated the weighty burdens these bishops were bearing. As we began the meeting, Bishop Shannon spoke first.

Bp Shannon: When I saw this on my calendar, I said, "Oh, yes. I can't wait to see my sisters. I don't care. To hear your voices too, and see your smiles." I'm dressed up because I had a TV interview. The unchurched state wants to know about what the Church is thinking.

Bp Kym: Oh my gosh. I had like five minutes with Phoebe and Carlye in my little prayer group and I was like, "Yes."

As leaders in their diocese, the pressure to respond—to offer some sense of hope—to the communities at large was felt acutely. I was astounded by their ability and willingness to stand as a bridge between their own raw grief and God's grace. Part of the challenge was that all of the members of the diocese were not of one mind. One bishop reported that a parishioner had announced imminent departure from the Episcopal Church. The interviews with Bishop Budde had led a parishioner to announce leaving the Episcopal Church because "we're all just a bunch of Trump-hating liberals." It became clear that the bishops were struggling with how to live into the call of leadership during these unprecedented times.

Bp Shannon: I just finished a call with my clergy too, because now they're wanting to do something—they're wanting to have not just one-offs. They want to do something that's ongoing to address racism and all of these things. But making that adjustment while we're in confinement is a little difficult.

Bp Phoebe: You know, I didn't say anything about all that is going on for about a week, so I think a lot of my people were glad that I finally said something, but it's just—we have to process everything. Like, I can't. I'm not a machine. I'm hurting too, you know.

Bp Carlye: I talked with the clergy today. I said there were two nonnegotiables we must observe. We needed to protect people over seventy-five. While over sixty-five is high risk, but for those over seventy-five, people get COVID and die. And then I said that we need to protect African Americans. I got those two words out of my mouth and couldn't say another word. Lost my stuff. Totally lost it. Just held silent, thinking, *You will not cry. You will not cry.* And then finally went, *Oh, you're getting ready to cry. That's getting ready to happen. It's a question of are you going to ugly cry, or are you going to professional woman cry? Which cry is it going to be? Because you're getting ready to cry in front of all the clergy.*

Bp Kym: I don't think a day went by last week I didn't cry. I mean, honestly, I don't think a day went by that I did not cry.

Bp Shannon: I have tried not to, which is why I couldn't say anything for a whole week.

Bp Phoebe: Exactly. That's why I didn't say anything either.

Bp Shannon: Because I just thought that if I let myself go to that space, I don't know if I can come back for them, for these people in my own house. My daughter just finished the eleventh grade and she had projects to finish. And I thought, *Okay, I don't have time to go there.* You know, my dad is a birder and so it started to slip.

At this point, I shared my own experience of being married to a Black man during this time. I had learned from my husband that Black men were beginning to ask one another when was the first time that they had been stopped by the police. My husband relayed three instances to me—two I knew about, but the third one I had never heard before. My brother-in-law's first experience was at the age of five. I asked the bishops how they were able to hold it all together and be a leader.

Bp Kym: For me, it's part of this whole piece of how the narrative of this culture has been so entrenched that any Black or Brown male over the age of five is a threat. I mean, that's what we live with and we experience it in education and we experience it in law enforcement. We experience it in every section of our life that our Black and Brown boys are somehow dangerous.

Bp Phoebe: The other thing that I'm having difficulty with is all the people who are saying, "Yes, we're for the peaceful protesters, but we don't support looting or violence." And I'm thinking, the footage I saw from the 1960s had a whole lot of Black folks dressed up in their Sunday best peacefully protesting. And what they were met with were dogs, fire hoses, Bull Connor [Theophilus Eugene "Bull" Connor, then commissioner of public safety for Birmingham, Alabama], and batons. Nobody supports looting and yet I don't think there's any form of protest that's acceptable anymore.

Bp Kym: No. Because clearly, you know, kneeling is out.

Bp Phoebe: Right.

Bp Kym: Using your voice at the Oscars is out.

Bp Phoebe: Right.

Bp Kym: Using your voice as an athlete is out.

Bp Phoebe: Right.

Bp Kym: Because the truth is the message is just shut up and be grateful.[7] And I have to say there was a part of me that just says, "Oh yes, Lord, help me to gird up my loins (Job 38.3 [KJV]) for what's coming."

Bp Shannon: I worried about what I had to say in the letter that went out. And it is part of why I was so strong and really clear about stating that this is evil, just calling it what it is, was because I was hearing from my clergy and laypeople.

A reporter asked me this afternoon, "So have you had anybody have a problem with what you said?" No, I haven't. I've only had people thank me. I know of one instance of a parishioner but mostly he was arguing over whether people were tear-gassed or whether it was just smoke.

And then I had another reporter ask me, "So when you're talking about these things, is it hard for you if the white people don't get it?"

I said, "Well, it's not even a matter of 'don't get it.'" My people say, "Yes, maybe we don't get it, but it doesn't matter whether we get it or not. It's not right. That's what's most important: that it's not right." They want someone to stand with them to say that it's not right. It's just sort of awkward being the voice for white people and I'm Black.

Concerns were also raised about raising children and about family members in such a toxic environment. In her homily delivered on May 31, 2020, Bishop Kym noted that her teenage son had prodded her two days prior with "Nothing's going to change is it, and what is the Church going to do about it?" I had watched her sermon on social media and it had brought me to tears.

Because this was our first session since March, I wanted to be sure to invite any topics they would like to discuss in future sessions. I had my own ideas, but it was important to provide a platform for them to engage in a dialogue about what they wished to discuss. First on their list was to talk about their own experiences of growing up in or around a Black church, and I promised that would be the agenda for our next meeting.

Cognizant of the preciousness of their time (we only allotted forty minutes for our reconnecting), Bishop Jennifer raised a powerful concept of just who is "the Church" which—while not addressed during this meeting—will be an underlying theme over the coming months.

Bp Jennifer: I'm interested in the word—the pronoun—"we." Let's unpack that and say who's the "we" in any given moment? It's just interesting because you have to parse your words and really ask questions about what people's assumptions are. And so, we are leading a predominantly white church in these times when there are a whole bunch of assumptions that people make. You need to ask and be curious, and not assume that the "we" implies anything unless it's been explicitly unpacked.

Bishop Jennifer's question helped to solidify that our conversations would not just be a "fellowship time." There definitely was a greater purpose for our time together, and we all shared an expectation that God had brought them to this time in history and would use them.

Holy and gracious God, we give you thanks for this time, for this project, and for the ability to speak, continuing to speak our truth into the world. We do so with humility and in expectation that you will use our experience, our stories, and our words in ways that will continue to bear fruit in our time in our places of ministry and that your Spirit will continue to move amongst the people. We ask that you would give us in this time the gift of rest, good sleep. Help us to see Sabbath as resistance and to help shore us up for the work ahead. In Christ we pray, Amen.

THE RT. REV. JENNIFER BASKERVILLE-BURROWS

Chapter 2

GROWING UP BLACK IN THE CHURCH

Setting the Scene

June had been a busy month for the country, the bishops, and their dioceses. The Black Lives Matter protests had been occurring across the country, with an estimated 15 million to 26 million people participating in demonstrations over the death of George Floyd.[1] The white police officer in the George Floyd case had been charged with second-degree manslaughter and second-degree murder.

Meanwhile, COVID-19 had now resulted in 2.5 million cases and over 125,000 deaths.[2] Some of the states were beginning to slowly open up or to reverse course, depending on how the pandemic was affecting their states; and the five bishops were issuing or updating guidelines, as needed.

On June 3, Bishop Jennifer released revised guidelines for diocesan churches in Indianapolis. "As anticipated, our understanding of COVID-19, the risks to our congregations in gathering, and the availability of reliable data have quickly evolved. The revision incorporates this evolution and helps to clarify my expectations in the regathering plans."[3] On the very same day, Bishop Kym issued a message regarding the Season II Transition, which was to begin on June 5, urging "caution as we move forward and that we continue to use technology as much as possible."[4]

On June 18, the Diocese of Vermont, under the leadership of Bishop Shannon, announced that the Restart Team had developed a five-phase plan, and the diocese was in Phase 1 of this plan, with their buildings closed and in-person worship suspended. Congregations could begin to develop and then submit plans for Phase 2, which allowed for building use by clergy, staff, and wardens only. On June 23, Bishop Carlye issued a thirty-six-page document for the Diocese of Newark, containing guidelines for in-person worship.[5] Bishop Phoebe had yet to issue any changes to the May 7 plan for the Diocese of West Tennessee, but these changes would be provided later in August.

The Conversation Begins

Our second virtual meeting was held on June 30, 2020. The women had expressed a desire to tell their stories of growing up Black in church. I posed a question for them to consider when sharing their experience: how did growing up Black inform your own faith journey and call to leadership?

While understanding that each would have a different experience, I hoped to find some common threads that seemed to weave together their stories. The bishops did not wish to have their biographies included in the book because their biographies were already readily available. But their stories would offer new insights into their own spiritual formation. And it was also clear that they would be hearing one another's stories for the very first time. They might know highlights or bits and pieces, but this was the first time to share with one another more about their experiences growing up. Bishops Phoebe, Carlye, and Jennifer grew up with a Black church experience.

Bp Phoebe: I was raised in a bicultural family, I guess. My mother's family is Episcopalian. My great grandfather Layton and my great grandfather Anderson were both on the faculty at St. Paul's College in Lawrenceville, Virginia. My grandmother was born in faculty housing and my grandparents knew one another from when they were children running around on that campus. So, I'm fourth-generation Episcopalian on my mother's side of the family. One of my mother's first cousins was an Episcopal priest and served mostly in the Chicago area.

My father's family is missionary Baptist. My grandfather was illiterate until his children went to school and he only learned to read as an adult. He was a sharecropper, and ended up being a deacon in that church.

My dad was one of nine—six who lived in Pine Bluff, one who lived in Chicago, one who was in Los Angeles, and one who was in Detroit. So, most of my extended family was at Indiana Street Missionary Baptist Church. Most Sundays the six of us [my parents and the four children] would go to Grace Episcopal and my mom and my three younger siblings would go on home. By the time my dad and I got to my grandparents' church at 11:30, they were just finishing up praise and worship. So, I grew up in both churches, and I know all those hymns. That music speaks to me.

Bp Carlye: One of the blessings of growing up in a segregated neighborhood in the '60s and '70s was the neighborhood really and truly was a family. Everybody knew everybody. And everybody's kid was everybody's kid. So, there was all this kind of support, affirmation, and authority to remind you of who you were if you needed to be reminded. At that particular time too, I think it was because of the civil rights movement in particular, but also it was how you saw your friends on the weekend.

We would get home from our church (which was early) and my next-door neighbors were just coming home for lunch before heading out to afternoon church. We kids would go with the neighbors to afternoon church. Some Sundays we would come back home from afternoon church and my parents would then want to go hear their favorite Black preacher on Sunday night. There were some Sundays where we did church all day long.

Being in and out of so many churches—so Baptist and so Holiness—I had a lot of Holiness friends. I didn't really know too many in the Pentecostal church, but I did experience a lot of Baptist churches and a number of Holiness churches. I have this very clear memory of my sister and I going to church with a friend and her mother. They were having a revival and special prayers before the revival. Everybody got down on their knees and turned into the pew. They were kneeling and facing the pew and everybody was huddled over their pew. I remember how my sister and I looked at each other and went: "We're the kneelers!"

And my friend's mother kept asking for an "Icee." She kept saying, "I want an Icee. I want an Icee. I want an Icee." My sister and I finally asked our friend afterward, "Why didn't your mom just go get an Icee? She kept saying she wanted an Icee." And our friend said, "She was praying." I kid you not, I was sitting in seminary thirty years later and they started talking about glossolalia and I'm like, *holy moly, that was our friend's mom!* She was praying in tongues. But I didn't have any vocabulary for that back then. I didn't know what that was, so I tried to make sense out of what I thought I had heard: "I want an Icee." All those years later I still remember her prayer and my first experience of a prayer language.

Bp Jennifer: It's funny, I hear lots of commonalities. I grew up in New York City in the borough of Brooklyn until I was ten years old, then we moved to the borough of Staten Island, where I lived until I went to grad school. My family is still there. I grew up thinking all the world's a diverse rainbow in Brooklyn because I lived in a very integrated neighborhood, housing projects that were integrated, and went to a very fantastic elementary school that I loved. It was a school where I had Black, Puerto Rican, and white teachers. Then I got to Staten Island and found myself in an environment that I later understood to be structural racism.

I didn't attend church though, I wanted to go, begged to go, and wanted to be baptized. My family didn't go to church. And so, my first church experience was the AME Zion church that was across the other street from our building in Staten Island. We could walk—I could get there by just crossing a very small street—and that's where all my friends went. That's really my first real church community experience.

While in junior high school, I was not going to church, but I was trying to figure out how to create a world where being Black or being white didn't matter. I just had such a rough time with trying to be friends with all kinds of people just because they were nice people. Having friends who were racially different wasn't politic.

Bishops Shannon and Kym grew up in a different church background than the others.

Bp Shannon: The church that I was going to was not a Black church, so there is not a Black experience for me. I always felt odd as a Black person living in Detroit because early on I was going to a school that my mother started.[6] I did interact with other Black people once I got to middle school.

Growing up, we lived in an intentional Christian community, all worshiping at the same church, where everyone shared everything in common (i.e., finances, housing, food, cars) as taught in Acts 4:32–35. We were part of other Christian communities living through the same experience as ours that were not necessarily Episcopalian. So while I grew up in a Black neighborhood, I don't have a Black experience in a church. I would say that a lot of the members were white and they were transplants. We used the hymnal rarely, but we did have lots of people that wrote music in the congregation. And so, it was different, but we did eventually, somewhat at the urging of my dad and of other Black members, started singing gospel music. We would just use whatever we chose. We didn't wait for anybody to approve it. I also was part of a gospel choir when I was a teenager.

My mother's mother was AME, but I never went to church with her. When I would go to church with my father's mother (who was I don't know what), people were falling out. I was praying, *Oh, God, please don't let that happen to me. Oh, my God. Just let me get through the service. Please don't let it happen.* It didn't.

When I was in high school, our church was very diverse. But then the race issue came up. It wasn't so much about women; our church would use inclusive language in the hymns so that it wasn't just about me. But then race became an issue, and I just decided that I couldn't go to this church with these people. I'm going to be Buddhist, bye. And my parents said, "Okay." There was no argument. But talking to Jesus doesn't work with Buddhism, so I let it go.

Bp Kym: I grew up in small town North Carolina outside an army base, Fort Bragg. And so, I had this very multicultural upbringing. On one side of me, I had neighbors where a Black guy was married to a woman from Germany. On the other side of me, I had neighbors where a Black guy was married to a woman from Thailand. My friends were this sort of melting pot.

I always talk about how I had a weird Southern upbringing because the high school I went to was built in conjunction with Fort Bragg Army base, so that all the kids who lived on base could go to the same school. It was the first integrated high school in Fayetteville. And I lived in Spring Lake, which is about twenty miles away—which meant I bussed there.

My childhood experience growing up was not being Black enough.[7] I mean, I had pigtails that hung down my back that got pulled often. My kids would ask me: "Mom, did you get into fights?" I was like, "Yeah, I did. I got into fights growing up." My family was like, "Nobody gets to tell you how Black you are. Nobody gets to tell you that."

After my godmother died, my stepfather was AME and he decided we should go to church as a family. So, I started going to the AME church and that was a place I didn't have to prove how Black I was because that was where I was accepted. And it was an odd experience for me because I never felt like I was Black enough except in that church environment.

While their growing up experiences may have been varied, they all embraced the Episcopal Church.

Bp Phoebe: People in Arkansas didn't know what it meant to be Episcopalian, and they didn't necessarily understand why I was in the Episcopal Church. But both sets of my grandparents were foundational in my life.

Because my parents had agreed that the children would be baptized and confirmed as Episcopalians, we'd all go to an Episcopal church at 10:00 a.m. I was born in March and baptized in June. I don't have any early memories of another church really except the Episcopal Church.

Bp Carlye: I grew up in the Episcopal Church in a Black Episcopal church. My mom was Roman [Catholic]. My dad was Baptist. And for the first few years I think we went to both. But once there were four of us kids, my parents decided that they needed to make a decision. One of my mother's best friends went to this Episcopal church; after my parents spoke with the priest, they thought they would give it a try. I don't remember any churches that we went to beforehand because I don't think we spent much time in them.

I love thinking about the church I grew up in. I remember the sound of ladies' girdles. To me, that was the sound of Sunday morning: swish, swish, swish, swish. And if they were in a rush: swish, swish, swish, swish, swish, and the heels clacking. I mean, I just thought that was a grown-up lady sound and I could barely wait to get a girdle and wear high heels, neither of which I ever did do. At six feet tall, I can never keep my balance in high heels. And then girdles were out by the time I was old enough to wear one, but I so aspired to that. I was completely doted on in that church.

Bp Jennifer: In my high school senior year, I went on a field trip—I had done a lot of leadership things and was president of a New York State Leadership Club. We went to DC for state officer training and that's where I had my conversion experience in St. John's Lafayette Square. I'd always wanted to go to church and I still hadn't found any place that felt right. The orthodox Jewish English teacher I had in eighth grade, Ms. Horowitz, had us read a play that talked about the Episcopal Church. And I remembered the name "Episcopal." So, when I had the choice to go to a church, I went to St. John's Lafayette Square and had a mystical-like experience, sensing that God was saying to me, "This is where you belong. This is your home." And that's when I started going to the Episcopal Church.

At that point, I was the only Episcopalian in my family. As I shared earlier, we were not churched and were more spiritual. If anything, we were more influenced by Native American spirituality, for my grandfather had grown up on the Shinnecock Reservation out on Long Island. And, after going to a Roman Catholic elementary school, my mother had an aversion to church in general. After I was in church for a while, she eventually was confirmed. But we are still the only two Episcopalians in our family that I know of. So, it's a real kind of an outlier thing. But nearly everybody else in my extended family goes to church. They just don't go to this church.

Bp Kym: My godmother, my mother's older sister, was the Episcopalian in the family. When she got back from Germany and found out I was two and hadn't been baptized, she decided that she had to fix that. So, that's when I became an Episcopalian.

St. Joseph's Episcopal Church was a Black parish. I remember beautiful Tiffany windows. It was classic Episcopalian. You know, that's where the doctors and the lawyers and the dentists—the Black ones at least—went to church. And church became a place where I didn't have to prove how Black I was; it was the place where I was accepted.

Bp Shannon: My dad [the Rev. Canon Ronald Spann][8] was Baptist as a boy. Someone brought him to sing as a soprano in the boys' choir at St. Andrew's in Ann Arbor, Michigan. That's how he came to the Episcopal Church. You know, they were not ordaining women back then, but women were always at the altar with my father doing something. So, as a child I thought I could become a priest.

Not surprisingly, all of the bishops were identified early as having leadership skills and special talents that prepared them for leadership roles in the Church.

Bp Carlye: When I look back at my church experience as a youngster, I'm sure I oversimplify some things, but it's just like a golden haze looking back into that. And yet, there is this interesting kind of twist on it all because of the problem with segregated schools at Fort Worth.

We lived in Oklahoma until I was five and then arrived in Fort Worth for the first grade. My grandmother was a first-grade teacher, so I finished kindergarten reading at the first grade reading level. But when I attended first grade in Fort Worth, in a separate but not equal school, I had lost a reading level. At that point, the Roman [Catholic] sisters had taken a strong stance toward integrating Black kids. They always had

Hispanic kids, but they were determined to take the Black kids in too.

This religious order came to Texas to integrate schools, so the Roman sisters knew what they were going to face. But it was also post–Vatican II, and there was a real sense of respect for the spirituality of the child. I was a really precocious spiritual kid and I was encouraged to be in charge of things. And so, they started helping me to plan liturgies beginning in third grade. By the fifth grade, I was planning liturgies for my class—and there was no one trying to get me to become Roman either. I was very active in my own Episcopal church; I started the Sunday school in my church. The Roman nuns even helped me figure out how to do the Sunday school in an Episcopal Church.

Bp Phoebe: As I grew older, I started doing lots of oratorical contests, speaking contests, and debating. The Episcopal priest who was the rector said, "You've got a wonderful voice and I want you to start reading scripture." And so, I became a lector at age fifteen, which was kind of unusual in the late '70s to have a girl that young on the rota. I think I was the only person who wasn't a grown adult on the rota. So, in both traditions my gifts were recognized and I had a lot of affirmation. I've probably been reading scripture in church for as long as I could read. And I wasn't necessarily a sacristy rat, but many of my friends who were AME, or AME Zion, or other sorts of Pentecostal, whenever their churches would have week-long revivals, they would say, "Well, come on, Phoebe, and come to church."

I was always in somebody's church, in somebody's revival, in a pickup choir, always around the church, again, with no thought that it would lead to anything beyond just my own spiritual edification. I guess to summarize, I grew up in the white Episcopal Church but also had the Black Baptist Church background. I have no memories of a time without God in my life.

Bp Kym: It's funny, Phoebe, that you would talk about doing speech and debate. I was doing that in high school too. And when my pastor at the AME church heard that I had won second place at state, he said to me, "You have a gift. I think you need to use it, so you're going to be preaching the youth sermon." So, for me, the AME Church was this affirmation of my gifts.

Bp Jennifer: During my brief time attending the AME Zion Church, I sang in the children's choir. I didn't like the worship because it was a little bit too Pentecostal charismatic for me. People were falling out all the time and the nurses would come and get people. And I just didn't get it, but I liked the choir. I liked to sing even though no one else wanted to hear me sing, but that was okay.

Outside of the church service, all the girls in the choir and the church youth program were really mean to me. It sounds like a really sad story, but it is true. I went to high school in Manhattan as a way to escape, having tested into a specialized school. I went off to Manhattan and discovered the world! I was with Blacks, Puerto Ricans, and whites— all of us with the aim to be the next person on Eyewitness News or the writer for the *New York Times* or whatever it was. That was our goal. When I got to high school in Manhattan, though, I had a robust and fabulous social life. And when people think about high school as something like would you repeat it, I'd go back tomorrow, every single day of it. It was that good. I didn't miss a day.

I began attending the Episcopal Church in college and by senior year had finally gotten up the nerve to go to coffee hour at the church that was in the middle of campus. Around that time, I began carrying in my wallet an article that was in *New York Magazine* about Chet Talton [the Rt. Rev. Chester L. Talton], then the rector at St. Philips [1985–1990]. I thought, *Oh, here's a Black priest.* This article had come out months before I graduated from college and I held onto it.

I wouldn't be baptized until after I graduated and moved back to New York City. In my first year as a baptized Christian, I attended an UBE [Union of Black Episcopalians] at St. Phillips Harlem and met Cheryl Parris [the Rev. Cheryl A.E. Parris], and a whole new world opened up for me in the Episcopal Church. I felt immediately at home.

As we were finishing up our hour together, I summarized what I heard from these bishops. They were all very, very smart and inquisitive children. They all grew up with a church experience, whether Baptist, AME, AME Zion, Episcopal, or Catholic. And a quest began early to discern the call deeply planted within. While a few of the bishops lived in a segregated environment growing up, by the time of college or graduate school, they were in a more integrated setting and were comfortable in diverse settings. Each of the women talked about how she felt affirmed in the Episcopal Church for her gifts and her talents—whether it was for singing, speaking, or as the lector/reader. Listening to each other's stories created a shared identity, a point of commonality, as they were affirmed early on for who they were and the possibilities of who they could become.

BpJennifer: The AME connection is a fascinating one here because I think there's a way which we don't talk about the AMEZ church or AME in our denomination. Yet, we are very linked with lots of crossover, but we don't talk about it very much.

Bp Shannon: Sometimes, I wish that I had a Black church experience. I was raised around protests, particularly for disarmament and antiwar, so it was a different experience. There were people living in our house that were not of the same family; we were community. We didn't even think about being Episcopalian that much.

Bp Carlye: When I look back at my life, there was an extraordinary village of people from all kinds of backgrounds that created the person I am today. I will call myself spiritually adventurous, definitely Christian. But even within the Christian lane, I'm very comfortable in a wide variety of settings. You want to pray in tongues, I'm in. I don't understand you and you don't understand me. But I have a prayer language. And if you want to adore the blessed sacrament, I will join you.

I appreciate the beauty found in a wide variety of worship traditions. So, there's just kind of a wideness of experience that I give credit to all those faithful people in my life growing up.

Bp Shannon: I hear this sense that even if you grew up in an Episcopal church there was always this sort of searching.

The bishops also began to talk about their early discernment process to priesthood and to discuss the gender gap in the Episcopal Church; both topics will be included in chapters 4 and 5. Clearly, there was much more to explore with the women about what it means to be a Black woman clergy in the Episcopal Church. Our time was coming to an end for this meeting. I looked forward to learning more about these daughters of the legacy of Bishop Barbara Harris of blessed memory. Bishop Jennifer offered the closing prayer.

Holy and gracious God, we give you thanks for this time, for your Holy Spirit that has been blowing amongst us and within us, working probably for decades to bring us to this moment. We ask your blessing as we depart and pray that your spirit in Christ will continue to hold us together until we gather again. Bless our work, our words, and our presence. In Christ we pray, Amen.

THE RT. REV. JENNIFER BASKERVILLE-BURROWS

Chapter 3

THE DUAL PANDEMIC

Setting the Scene

Representative John R. Lewis, a civil rights icon who was called the "conscience of Congress," died on July 17, 2020, and his widely televised funeral was to be held on July 30—the date of the next meeting with the five bishops. Lewis had written his final essay two days before his death, and had asked that it appear in the *New York Times* on the day of his funeral, imploring, "Though I may not be here with you, I urge you to answer the highest calling of your heart and stand up for what you truly believe."[1]

A little over two months had passed since the murder of George Floyd, and protests were continuing nationwide. While there had been some progress at the state and local levels (e.g., Minneapolis, Denver, Colorado, and Pennsylvania), police reform at the national level was stalled. On the opening day for the Major League Baseball season on July 22, both the Washington Nationals and the New York Yankees players knelt in support of Black Lives Matter.

With 150,283 US deaths and 4.41 million cases reported[2] COVID-19 is often reported as the "double pandemic." At the

House of Bishops meeting held virtually July 28–29, Presiding Bishop Michael B. Curry's sermon centered around the Holy Eucharist, racial reconciliation, communion, divine and human, in a time of pandemic.[3]

The Conversation Begins

Our discussion for this July 30 meeting was to focus on leading through the prism of the pandemic, the economic crisis, the growing acknowledgment of racial injustice, and the deepening political partisanship. Specifically, I was interested in how their lives have been affected during this time—both personally and as a diocesan bishop. What were they learning? And what did they believe was needed to make meaningful and lasting changes in this country and in the Church? Perhaps because they had just attended the House of Bishops meeting, foremost on the minds of the five women was their responsibilities as a bishop to respond to the pandemic.

Bp Jennifer: You know, it's an interesting question. After we understood that this pandemic was going to be lasting a lot longer than a couple months, which we kind of knew but didn't really know in our bones the way we know now, I find that the pace is unrelenting. But I also have more time for reflection.

When I started the year in January, I was feeling quite dry and uninspired; but now, in this pandemic time, I feel like there's been a crystallization and an urgency of the mission. That helps me to find it easier to write and to speak and to show up because there are so many essential things that need to be tended to that have coincided with the coronavirus pandemic.

And all of the heightened matters around racial injustice, police brutality, and the demise of our democracy makes it really clear for me about how it all impacts the gospel. It is my actual vowed vocation to speak and inspire to help gather people to respond to this moment as people of faith. It's not that I've dropped the ball on those other responsibilities, but I've gotten a lot clearer about delegating them or just not having to worry about them. There's so much more essential work and leading to be done; and I need to attend to people pastorally who are in my care.

So, I feel freed up a little bit to be really clear about that which is essential and about the things that I will not do just because I think it's a good thing for me to do. I'm probably still overcommitted in some ways than I would like to be, but I'm struggling less with myself about some of my choices.

I will say something different when we go back to school, so let me just qualify that. As we were starting this meeting, I received a letter from the head of the school where my son attends saying that we're still opening on August 13. But as God as my witness, if we go back to remote learning and I don't have my quarantine pod figured out, I'm going to be a hot mess. So, there it is.

Bp Carlye: I find that there's levels to this. On one hand, there is an acceptance of who I am within myself that is greater than I've ever experienced in my life—where I am not second-guessing myself. I'm not comparing my actions, reactions, or needs to anybody else's. I'm just 100 percent in my own world, in the present, available, and deeply connected to where God wants and needs me to be in this present moment.

And then on another level, I don't think I have ever been as distraught about where we are as a nation as I am now. I take it personally. I feel like somebody did this to my country. I have very young memories of being in odd places, being in military barracks in Ghana with the Girl Scouts when I was fifteen years old, and being with people who didn't know how they were going to get their next meal. I didn't remember where my passport was, and a Marine told me: "Don't you ever get separated from big blue. That thing is your ticket out of hell, no matter where you are in this world. It guarantees all that we hold dear as Americans." It's a simple statement, but it also gets at the heart of how I personally feel that somebody has attacked all that I hold dear as an American. And I'm shocked. I'm still shocked about it.

But it doesn't mean that I'm not resolute. It doesn't mean I'm not taking action. There's also the part of me that is relieved because I would always rather know the truth. There are kind of two places in my being: one that is incredibly distraught, and the other that is incredibly at peace and at one with where everything is.

I don't think people realize the ferociousness that comes along with my sense of peacefulness because they see my Christianity first. But there is a deep digging in what is going on within me to deal with things. To our diocese I say so often, in a very frank and blunt way at every opportunity: "We're only trying to do one thing right now, and that is bring an end to racism and an end to white supremacy in our corner of the world." A bold statement, but that's what we're trying to do. And that's a significant change. I wouldn't have said that six months ago. Now I say it at breakfast, lunch, and dinner.

BpPhoebe: Probably unique in the group, I had to self-quarantine in the middle of March because I shook a hand of someone who tested positive for COVID-19 at an event in St. Paul's Chattanooga. The rector has fully recovered, thanks be to God. Because of the self-quarantine, I was already aware of a lot of anxiety within myself, so I have found that I don't have a lot of patience for people who are pushing back about why we have to stop singing and why we have to wear a mask. Or saying, "Bishop, we're in a small rural area. We don't have COVID-19 out here."

There are a number of things in my diocese that were already on the horizon, but COVID has exacerbated and sped up the timeline. For example, now I have some of my clergy who have preexisting health conditions and are retiring earlier than anticipated.

Bp Kym: I have been pondering over the questions to be discussed today as well as the last time we talked together. Since then, several things happened. First, I participated in a round-table discussion at the College of Bishops. After I was asked how many years did I plan before my retirement, the facilitator reminded me that my task was to play the long game as a bishop. Then, in another conversation, I was reminded that I could not allow others to make me believe that I was called to this diocese to be anybody other than who I am. When I heard that, all the anxiety just fell away; it just dropped off my shoulders. That was really it, that my authenticity—who I am and how I live—is part of what they called. I was called to this place because of who I am and therefore I must lead the way I lead. And so, I am persistent in being real with folks, to always to talk about my politics grounded in the gospel.

BpShannon: Ever since I read the profile for my diocese, I had the feeling that this is really the place for me, that this is the place where I would feel most like myself and where I am called to be in ministry. As a new bishop, if I didn't feel so much like myself, it would have been so much more difficult to ask them to adhere to such stringent restrictions regarding COVID-19. There was a calling for us to respond as an entire diocese as we cared for our most vulnerable.

Of particular concern for the bishops was the growing division and politization across the country around wearing a mask to protect oneself and others from the coronavirus.

Bp Kym: While I was on vacation, the governor of Colorado's mask order went into effect statewide. My position was that we needed to remind our folks that our primary task is keeping folks safe; and that, at the very minimum, they must comply with state and municipal government orders. At the minimum, that's what they have to do, grounded in scripture because we always do.

I've said to my clergy, "I don't really see any point of telling grown folks what to do because grown folks will do whatever the heck they want to do. What I am asking you to do is to live into a notion of Church that is bigger than you, that our understanding of Church is more than 104,000 square miles of this state."

BpShannon: Most people understand that we need to do something. We need to make sure that we're not just focusing on Sunday morning, and to realize that it is going to be a cultural shift. But know that if you start having these conversations, there may be a group that wants to pull away from the Episcopal Diocese of Vermont.

I don't know, maybe I wouldn't have been so strong and clear in my conversations if there hadn't been a pandemic. We don't have time for foolishness and I'm not going to encourage it. And people are actually happy that I can say that, like you, I too am tired of wearing a mask all the time. But I wear a mask for your protection.

Bp Phoebe: I'm finding that I feel a sense of urgency that we need to get real about all of this. But to speak what is truth can result in a lot of backlash from others who aren't quite ready to say, "Yes, this is the truth." A lot of my good, faithful folks have been in denial and I would say that they can't continue to ignore it, even though they are trying to continue to ignore it.

When I, as their bishop, say, "Look, let's at least be honest about where we are," for some people it's reassuring. But for others, it just makes the anxiety level go even higher because they would like for me to help them be in denial, to pretend with them so that they will feel better. And I'm not going to do that.

So, I am also more self-aware about not so much the content of my message but how I deliver it. I have found that COVID-19, in addition to giving me clarity about a lot of things, has also caused me to reflect on my own leadership style, my own way of conveying information, and my own way of supporting the people who are around me so that they can be the best versions of themselves in this time of high anxiety and stress.

I raised the question again of who is "we"—which Bishop Jennifer had asked at our first meeting—when speaking of the Episcopal Church. Were they finding a new meaning evolving for "we" as a Black woman bishop? And what did they believe was needed to make meaningful and lasting change in the Church?

Bp Shannon: One thing that I think the Church needs is to have leaders that embody a different image of leader in their physical selves, people like us so that there's not just one type of leader in the Church. We can never be who we say we want to be if our leaders never look like somebody else, if they never look like Black women. That is part of my discernment during this time. How is the Church going to be this fuller picture of what we keep saying that we want to be? How can we be fully inclusive and nonracist in all the different ways that we dream about ourselves as Episcopalians?

Bp Phoebe: It seems to me that this crisis has further demonstrated the lack of discipleship, and the need for transformed hearts. There are a lot of good, faithful people who have been coming to church for forty years to check a box. They walk out of the nave on Sunday and they're living their country club lives until Saturday night. Then they begin to think about what they are going to wear to church the next day, rather than to think about the radical nature of Jesus's invitation to live into new life.

There needs to be additional work around formation and discipleship of adults. Maybe they did confirmation, Sunday school, J2A [Journey to Adulthood] with the youth pilgrimage, even college chaplaincy. But now they are busy working—with children or older parents needing their time.

I think about that parable of the various seeds, and I am not sure how many adults have roots that go deep. So, one of the things I'm really thinking about from a diocesan standpoint is how can we facilitate an intentional program of discipleship. I think that's maybe what the Church needs.

Bp Kym: I think you're right in terms of formation, Phoebe, on a huge scale. What is this life of baptismal calling? You say those words about your baptismal covenant, but do you have any intention of living them?

What we've been called to do is to live into this kingdom that we've been given a vision and a foretaste of. And if Eucharist has not been a call to you that we—to quote Mark Hollingsworth—have the goal of achieving communion, not receiving it,[4] then you have missed something. And I think that missing piece is becoming a very visible gaping hole in our ecclesiology and archeology.

Bp Jennifer: When I came to church in my early twenties, I went through baptismal prep that took three months. And then, for three and a half years—until I went to grad school—it was year-round Christian formation. I learned how to read the back of the hymnal; the politics of the church; and about antiracism. There was always Christian formation, always. And it wasn't like the entire congregation took part in it, but a good percentage did.

After I was ordained years later, I was a director of Christian formation at a parish, and we wrestled with how to provide formation for pre-K through ninety. We had a children sermon three Sundays out of four with a packed house with all of these kids. But the adults just wanted to have coffee hour; they were chatting and having a break from their kids.

And in order to keep people happy and coming, the church didn't say this is exactly what it means to be a follower of Jesus. We were unable to figure that out and I saw the future walking up to it. And now here we are.

I find that in this moment the people who are "all in" are the ones who have been "all in" all along. These are the communities that have taken that discipleship seriously, who have figured out a way to offer some kind of ongoing formation for adults so that they can mature in their Christian walk. Even if I don't agree with all that they're doing, I don't worry because I know that they can account for their faith in ways that they can articulate to the world And, that tells me that they are taking their faith walk seriously.

As bishops, we're living our formation while, at the same time, dealing with all of this stuff that's coming at us in this country at this moment. I hate the situation that we're in, honest to God. It's all too much all the time. And yet, I think: *what's our opportunity as the Church to actually take advantage of this moment to help give people what they need?* Because as horrific as it is, this will not be the last crisis we see in our episcopacy.

Yes, there may be some in the country club set who fall away. I hope that God blesses and keeps them, and that they find their way back to the community. But I also think the core will be strengthened. And hopefully, those who are really drawn to Christ and his word and those who want to reshape the entirety of their lives around the Good News will grow.

Bp Carlye: This is almost like the pre-formation issue which to me is conversion. I think we just aren't quite sure what we think about Jesus. And because we're not quite sure what we think about Jesus, then we're not quite sure what we think about a whole lot of other things. And so, I feel like this is a major conversion moment that we are in. I'm aware of people coming to God in a way that has not been described before. I feel God's presence in a way that I have never felt before.

We need to figure out a way to be together—and together doesn't necessarily mean on Sunday morning at 10:00 o'clock. The challenge in the United States is that we're so defined by our independence. That independence impacts people in churches because they're defined by their independence. But there is this thing, this sense of power, this unleashing that happens when we are united. I think converted people who learn how to be fully actualized in their faith can unite with other people to actually do something and change something just by their very presence.

I was struck by the bishops' raw openness and theological conclusions in the midst of all that was going on around them. There was such a sense of hope for the country, for the Church, and for the people entrusted in their care. As Bishop Shannon observed, "I think that there's something special about our leadership in this time because as Black women, we've experienced so much. And we still find hope. We're still hopeful people." Perhaps one of the greatest gifts received on that day was that inspired by Bishop Carlye's prayer to end our session, I found the title for this book.

Good and gracious God, we thank you for the gift of each other,
that in the absolute craziest time that I have ever experienced,
it feels like a personal gift to have this band of sisterhood that

completely gets it. I don't have to go into explanation, that they understand it all and that we are in it together. And we continue to give ourselves, our ministries, our families, our hopes, our dreams, our worries, our fears, and our challenges over to you. We know that you have called us specifically into this time; and that you have shaped us to be the people that we are at this very moment. And in all of this, we know that you have plans that will dazzle us. So, we look forward to seeing those plans and we trust you to continue to guide us. In Christ's name we pray, Amen.

THE RT. REV. CARLYE J. HUGHES

Chapter 4

DISCERNING THE CALL

In preparation for our upcoming meeting, I went back to review earlier comments made by some of the bishops regarding their own spiritual path—a winding road, indeed—during their college years. And at some point in time, someone else suggested, encouraged, or inspired them to consider answering a call to priesthood.

Bp Phoebe: One Sunday, early in my first semester at Harvard, I went to Memorial Chapel and heard Peter Gomes [the Rev. Peter J. Gomes] preach and said, "I'm home. I can do this for four years." And so, I sat at the feet of Peter Gomes for four years as a Harvard undergrad and that was just an amazing experience. After graduate school, I began my professional career in Richmond, Virginia, as a public policy analyst. In 1989, I joined St. Philip's Episcopal Church, 2900 Hanes Avenue, which is the church where, twenty-five years later, I became rector. But of course, when I was there the first time, I had no idea that ordination was anywhere in my future.

Bp Kym: I remember the day I left church and swore to God I was never going back. It was when I heard an associate pastor preach a sermon that was basically the equivalent of "if girls kept their legs closed there wouldn't be any teenage pregnancies." I walked out of church and swore that I was never going back ever again. But my college chaplain changed my mind and brought me back to the Episcopal Church.

Bp Carlye: I almost left church too. I say this and I know people think it is hyperbole, but it's not. When I moved to Boston for college and I was trying to find an Episcopal church, there was no Episcopalian presence on the campus. I visited several Episcopal churches, all with small and elderly white congregations.

I called my parents after a month and asked, "What happened to our church? Only elderly white people go to it up here. There are no Black people in these churches and aren't we a Black church? What happened to our church?" I mean, I genuinely had no experience of the dozens of white Episcopal churches in Fort Worth, Texas, because we were that segregated in the church. If you were Black and you showed up at another Episcopal church in Fort Worth, they would kindly steer you over to St. Simon's. "Get your Christian-self up out of here and go to the Black side of town."

Bp Kym: My chaplain at Wake Forest University, a white man, got me back into attending church. After I'd been in chapel for a year, he said, "I think it's time for you to be confirmed." I was like, "Great; I think I'm ready." After I got confirmed, about a year later my junior year, he asked, "Have you ever considered that you might be called to the priesthood?" And I said, "No. I've never considered that." He responded, "I think you might be." I'm like, "No, I'm not." But he just said, "Well, how about we just start discerning?" And I was like, "Okay."

While Bishop Shannon did not share about her college years during our virtual meetings, she does describe her Paul-like experience beautifully in her doctoral dissertation.

My resistance to God's nagging and directing was gone, at least on the part about going back to Detroit after graduation from college. I knew God wanted me to return for a purpose, but for what? I cannot say that I was afraid. But I was apprehensive . . . maybe better described as a combination of excitement, awe, and doubt. Ok, maybe a grain of fear. Even before this experience, God had spoken to me about a call to priesthood, but I was not ready to hear it. Over twenty years have passed since then. I took many different paths, all leading back to the first inkling of call I discerned at the age of six.[1]

Setting the Scene

Both the Democratic and the Republican conventions had ended, with then President Donald Trump and former Vice President Joseph [Joe] Biden Jr. now the nominees for the 2020 presidential election. On August 10, Joe Biden had selected Senator Kamala Harris as his running mate—the first Black woman and the first person of Indian descent—to be nominated for national office by a major party.

On August 23, Jacob Blake, a Black man living in Kenosha, Wisconsin, had been shot seven times in the back by a police officer. On August 28, a March on Washington, organized by political and civil rights leaders, was held on the same day that Dr. Martin Luther King Jr. delivered his "I Have A Dream Speech" fifty-two years prior.

Nightly protests had been occurring in Portland, Oregon, since the murder of George Floyd. On August 29, a caravan of trucks supporting "Trump 2020" clashed with protesters, and a man who was a member of the far-right group Patriot Prayer was killed by a gunshot wound to his chest. And, on September 11, the five former police officers with the Minneapolis Police Department appeared in court for the first time.

Supreme Court Justice Ruth Bader Ginsburg died on September 18 at the age of eighty-seven. Justice Ginsburg had a long history of voting for social issues, including affirmative action and women's rights. The Senate Majority Leader Mitch McConnell had announced that he would quickly move to replace the open seat, which would bring the total to three Supreme Court Justices appointed during the Trump administration.

Meanwhile, the United States had surpassed 6 million COVID-19 cases, and one of the White House's medical advisers was proposing "herd immunity" (allowing the coronavirus to spread throughout the population quickly).[2]

The Conversation Begins

With all that was going on in the country, I wondered if we would be able to focus on our meeting topic: the discernment process to enter a diocesan bishop search. It was the first day back to work for both Bishop Jennifer and Bishop Shannon after their vacations.

Bp Jennifer: My heart is in a good place. What I've been saying is I'm rested, but I'm not reinvigorated. I'm healthy, but I'm not energized. It's just the season we are in.

Bp Shannon: I found it took forever to just take my mind out of the space of what was going to meet me when I got back. Three weeks in, I thought, *Wow, I don't think this is going to happen.* But then I let that go, and I felt a little better.

As the bishops joined the virtual meeting and I listened to their greetings to one another, I began to wonder how much more of their time I reasonably could ask for to complete the book. Ideally, I wanted one more session, but if that were not possible, I offered to meet with them individually.

Bp Kym: Well, I know it's really hard to wrangle us because our schedules are just that insane. But for me, it is just a gift to see your guys' faces.

Bp Carlye: And truth be told, we don't get to hear each other's stories. It's rare that we have had the chance to just tell these stories.

The questions planned for this meeting were to be centered around the bishops' discernment process to enter a diocesan bishop search. After all, they were among the few Black bishops in the Episcopal Church. Among the active bishops (diocesan, suffragan, assistant, or assisting), fourteen were Black men and six were Black women.[3] Specifically, I wondered if they thought that there are any unique qualities, preparation, or experiences needed for a Black woman to consider. As I listened to them, I was struck by how each spoke about a call to discernment to leadership rather than a call to be bishop. Their attention and prayer life were focused more on discerning whether or not they were being called to pursue more of a leadership role in the Church. Through their own discernment processes, each realized how important it was to be authentic and to be true to who she was. Most importantly, the Holy Spirit was so fully in their discernment process, that this released them from any concerns about the outcome.

Bp Phoebe: As far as the basic discernment, I think it was like the discernment for ordination in general. It was talking with a small group of trusted friends, mentors, and family members for their honest assessment about whether or not they thought I had the gifts to even do this. I also spoke with my spiritual director, and I engaged in a lot of listening. I finally decided that it was important for me to commit to the process and not to be so worried about the particular outcome. I believed that I was going to learn something about myself, and I would learn a lot more about this church that I love— just from opening myself up.

When I was in that narrowing down phase, a Black clergy reminded me that it had only been a year since Jennifer had been elected. And that it had been five years before another Black person was elected; and before that there was a gap of ten to fifteen years. I was told that right now, the system is full. I remember walking away thinking, *Unless, of course, that's what God wants.*

Bp Kym: I entered two bishops' election processes—Utah and North Carolina—and was not moved forward. But then I joined a group whose desire was to encourage women of color to enter bishops' processes. And so, I dedicated myself to that because I felt that was a good way for me to spend my energy and offer my support. I remember sitting in the room with several of my Black women clergy colleagues and the facilitator read the profile for Colorado. She asked my colleagues, "So who do you think that sounds like?" And they all said that it sounds like Kym.

As I was writing my answers, I'd send them to friends and colleagues. They told me that wasn't me, that I needed to show them who I really am. They were right. If I was going to be a part of this process, I needed to be fully and authentically myself. That gave me the freedom to really write my theology and my understanding of my baptismal covenant; and who I believe we are called to be as Church.

Bp Carlye: The church community was a powerful force in my discernment. The community saw things that I could not picture for myself. A friend in my parish suggested I think about seminary. A trusted clergy friend asked me to think about the episcopacy

I have found I needed to be talked into this every step of the way. I have a very active imagination when thinking about the possibilities for other people, ministry, the Church. But when it comes to myself, I become practical and pragmatic. I knew what priests looked like. In my case, they were usually from Scotland or Ireland because back home our parish priest was Scottish and the priests I grew up with first grade through twelfth grade were all Irish Catholics. All the priests knew I was a really spiritual kid, but they were men and so for me, that's what priests looked like. And I wasn't trying to be the Queen of England either.

I have to say for the bishop process, the other thing that slowed me down more than anything is that I am from the Episcopal Church. I haven't known anything else. And the way we tell a priest "you are good at your job" is to say, "You are going to be a bishop one day."

So, when people first started talking to me about being bishop, I said, "Thank you," or "You're welcome," because I knew they were saying, "Hey, well done."

I remember looking at bishops and thinking that it was a hard job. We don't pay them enough. They don't have enough authority. They don't have enough resources and everybody expects that they're going to walk on water and make the whole diocese walk on water with them. So, it had no appeal to me at all.

In my last diocese, my bishop [the Rt. Rev. James Scott Mayer] sat and talked with me over and over again. Finally, he said, "There's one thing that I don't think you understand. The Church is full of people who can do things. When you talk, people want to get up and move. We don't have that many people who inspire people and the Church needs people like that right now." He continued, "It makes more sense to put that resource in a place where it reaches more people and can potentially mobilize things on a larger level"—to which I thought, *Okay, now that starts to make sense.*

Bp Jennifer: My whole discernment in the ministry has always been about really listening. Folks often said that they thought I should be a bishop. Some folks questioned and asked why I was taking various calls in ministry [like serving as a university chaplain]. I truly felt called to those positions, and I was doing the hardest work yet the most gratifying work.

Like Carlye, I heard really early that I would be a great bishop; it seemed like a really easy way for people to compliment my ministry. I remember hearing that in 2000 when I had been a priest for only three years.

I was grateful for the recognition, but I didn't feel like I could put a lot of credence in it as something meaningful. Then Rochester came open, so I thought, *Well, maybe I should investigate it.* I did not get past the first step, and I thought, *Well, there's that.* Many years later, other bishop processes came open in places I had served, like Central New York (I didn't think I'd go home again) or places I wanted to be, like Western North Carolina.

I went to General Convention [governing body of The Episcopal Church] in 2015 thinking maybe I can still be open to this discernment about Western North Carolina. The convention came and went, and it was after I got back home to Chicago that Indianapolis had put out its profile; and I began getting calls about Indianapolis. I finally looked at the diocesan profile for Indianapolis, and was so excited by it, that over two days I spent all-nighters, getting my stuff together to finally get it submitted the day before the deadline.

Bp Shannon: I think that my discernment about being a bishop began when I was in the Diocese of Michigan and was the rector of this historic Black church. I was the first woman rector and so often finding myself just being the only one wherever I was, in a predominantly Black city. Even when I went into ecumenical settings, I was the only woman in the room all of the time. This sense of invisibility became this big hurt within me for Black Episcopal churches.

And so, as I began my doctoral studies and found some grounding in womanist theory. I realized that what I was experiencing wasn't just to help myself but to help my congregation and to help the whole Episcopal Church. If the Episcopal Church is going to be what it wants to be, then the leadership needs to look more like what we're saying we want to be. From that research, I decided I was going to do all I could to be part of the group of women with whom I could partner to grow that leadership in more visible ways for the Church. And I also realized that if I was going to really get behind that, I would have to allow myself to be in places where I wouldn't be just with Black people; because the Episcopal Church isn't just made up of Black people.

My mentor—who is a priest and a white woman—told me that I should be a bishop. That was not my aspiration, even as a priest. After I began actually to take the bishop process seriously, I just thought, *I'll do it.* But I was really nervous about opening myself up to having people putting me on the spot.

After I read the profile [for the Diocese of Vermont], I decided that it was worth entertaining the idea. There were things I thought that I could bring to this particular diocese. But I also was not going to be anybody else but myself. At a certain point, I just decided not to worry about those steps that I would have to go through until I got to them. I'm just going to take this moment and this time, write my materials, and hope that it goes well.

While I had hoped that the bishops would discuss any particular skills needed for preparing for participation in the diocesan bishop process, the only topic they spent any time on was the walkabout. During the process of electing a new diocesan bishop, a walkabout (i.e., walking tour) is required so that the candidates can mingle with members of the Church throughout the diocese. These walkabouts usually include a presentation with a question and answer opportunity.

Bp Phoebe: I wasn't even convinced that I was going to win. Like, I didn't think I was going to win after the walkabouts, but just deciding to be honest, to be myself and to put it all on the line.

Bp Carlye: Actually, Newark was my test run at walkabouts. My husband told me that if I didn't get elected to this, I was on my own. He wasn't coming back for any more of those things. I asked him why he thought I would put myself through that again? This was a one and done. Let's get home in one piece as fast as we can!

Bp Shannon: I remember looking at Carlye's walkabout videos. I thought, wow, I could do that because she looked like she was being herself. I also remember sending Kym a note when she was about to go on her walkabouts, telling her that I was going to be at her ordination. She says, "Yeah, yeah, I'm just going to walkabout."

Bp Jennifer: I didn't want to do this [become a bishop] if I was not going to be able to enjoy my life. Life is too short. I remember going into the walkabout in Indianapolis and thinking, *Well, I'm not sure if this is it still, but I'm discerning and I'm open.* By the end of the walkabouts, the idea of serving in Indianapolis became my reason for living.

Bp Kym: My walkabout was 5,000 miles over mountains and through woods. When I arrived in Colorado Springs, there were over 200 people there. And the only people of color in the room were myself and the representative from the diocesan search committee. There were two candidates with two sessions each. I remember going into the room after my first session and saying to my husband, "I cannot do this again. It's too much. I'm too tired." I really was just tapped out.

Then my husband said, "You know what, I'm still going to go home with the hottest person in this room." About then I realized that my mic was still on! But it was enough of an adrenalin rush to get me through the next session. I remember praying the same prayer that I prayed to Jesus when I was waiting for the standing committee to come back with whether I was a candidate for ordination or not. And I was like, "Okay, Jesus, this is it. I'm done. This is your shot and I'm not doing this again."

The five bishops expressed gratitude for the white women who not only organized programs for women clergy but who also advised them personally during the bishop process.

Bp Jennifer: In 2016, there was no other Black woman diocesan to be that representative figure for me, but there was all this other conversation among women in general. The purple scarf day at General Convention [2015] was an impactful moment.[4] In Salt Lake City, there was this whole conversation beginning about women in the episcopacy and trying to shift the tide of women in elections.

When I decided to enter the bishop process for Indianapolis, people said to call Chilton Knudsen.[5] She coached me every step of the way and helped me to see from a woman's perspective what it would mean to be a diocesan bishop. Longtime mentor Gayle Harris [a Black woman] also guided and coached me as I discerned in this bishop search.

Bp Phoebe: I participated in Beautiful Authority that Mary Gray-Reeves convened in California.[6] That was for all women, not just women of color, to consider higher level positions, which are cardinal rector, canon to the ordinary, dean of a cathedral, and episcopate. You would go to these conferences and women in those four roles led workshops on how they got to where they were. You then could decide in which of those tracks you wanted to participate. I went to the one on the episcopate and it just sounded crazy, but canon to the ordinary made a lot of sense because I was an attorney before seminary. So, I think my first inkling of something more than rector was to be canon to the ordinary. At the time, there was no Black woman who was canon to the ordinary in the country. And I thought, that's something that I could do.

Bp Shannon: I met with Helen Svoboda-Barber at Leading Women[7] because I had applied for her first cohort, but it was filled. She told me that she had been trying to get together a group of Black women or women of color because she imagined that we probably had different concerns and issues. She asked me to help her find some women for the group. We were the only group that she had of color.

Throughout the conversations, Bishop Jennifer's name was mentioned often. As the first Black woman consecrated as a diocesan bishop, she was an inspiration for and mentor to the other four bishops. Their deep gratitude and affection for Bishop Jennifer blazing the trail—and "lifting as we climb"[8]—was shared by them all. And it was Bishop Phoebe's tribute to Bishop Harris, the "mother" of the legacy, that inspired the words for the dedication of this book.

Bp Phoebe: I want to start because the reason that I'm here, I'm looking at her. And that's Jennifer Baskerville-Burrows.

Until Jennifer was consecrated diocesan, I never would have considered any episcopal election. It just seemed like an exercise in futility to me. There had only been two Black women, and your last name had to be Harris, and you had to be willing to go to Massachusetts, and you had to be willing to be a suffragan.

Having lived in Cambridge for four years, I wasn't interested in going back to Boston. So, it really was Jennifer having the courage and the strength that even allowed me to think about it. Not only did I fight the call to the priesthood but also very much fought the call to the episcopate. Had Jennifer not won, I could not have seen myself in this role.

I think that probably the most important thing for me was to see how Jennifer was able to envision herself in a role that had never been occupied by somebody who looked like her. Then I remember so clearly going to Carlye's consecration in September of 2019, on the same day that it was announced that I was on the slate for West Tennessee. A photo was taken of Jennifer, Bishop Barbara of Blessed Memory [Bishop Barbara Harris], Kym, Carlye, and me. I remember that as a highlight.

Bp Carlye: You [Jennifer] were the only person I talked to about walkabouts beforehand. There was a man who talked to me about campaigning that raised some questions within myself. That phone call with you was so helpful.

Bp Kym: When the profile for Colorado came out, I thought, I'm not really into this. So, I pouted about it. I prayed about it. And then Jennifer called me and bullied me into applying. She told me that she had read the profile and that I had to say "yes."

I have to say I was so deeply grateful for Jennifer already having had the experience [of being in the episcopal process]; and of talking with me about discernment. Every step of the way is about discernment, discerning whether you are called to lead, and whether you can be with these people and love them.

Bp Shannon: I remember telling Jennifer, as we prepared for her consecration, "I cannot do this." We were eating breakfast and she says, "Oh, don't say that. It's not that bad." I'm thinking, *She's crazy, but I'm glad she's here.*

In the time allotted, we never did address the question of whether they believed there are any unique qualities, preparation, or experiences needed for a Black woman to consider in a discernment about a diocesan bishop process, but in a future session they did speak extensively about what it is to a Black woman clergy. Bishop Kym offered the closing prayer for this day.

Gracious God, in this moment where there is so much strife, in this moment where there is so much struggle, I give you thanks. Thanks for this calling and thanks for these companions with whom I walk. I pray for your Church, the Universal Church and for the Episcopal Church, that we might find our way to you amidst all the brokenness and the pain in this world. I ask that you keep our hearts tender, that we always see the suffering around us and that we speak your grace into those places of suffering. That you give us your wisdom as we lead your people, that by your grace we may overcome the deep divisions that threaten our Church and our world. I thank you for all of the blessings this day that we will receive, those we will notice and those we won't recognize. And thank you for your continued presence with us through our Lord Jesus Christ. Amen.

THE RT. REV. KIMBERLY (KYM) LUCAS

Chapter 5

LIVING INTO THE CALL

Setting the Stage

Our fourth meeting was held on October 13, 2020. On that day, the United States resumed the number one position globally for daily incidences of the COVID-19 pandemic, now up to 59,699 new cases per day, the highest since August 3.[1] On October 2, President Donald Trump was hospitalized for the coronavirus and was released three days later.

Since our meeting a little over a month prior, a lot had happened in the country. On September 23, the grand jury in the Breonna Taylor case failed to charge any of the white police officers who were involved with her killing on March 23 when they forced entry into her apartment. Protests broke out across the country. On October 9, the second presidential debate between the President Donald Trump and Vice President Joe Biden had been cancelled. The confirmation hearings were to begin on October 14 for Supreme Court nominee Amy Coney Barrett to fulfill the seat left by the death of Justice Ruth Bader Ginsburg on September 17.

This was to be our last scheduled meeting. The bishops had either completed or were about to hold their diocesan conventions. Over the months we had spent together, it was evident to me that these exceptional, extraordinary Black women leaders knew that their words mattered and had no desire to cause any harm to the Church that they so dearly loved. As honest and authentic Black women leaders, they were always spiritually grounded in their responses to my questions.

While our discussion for this session was to focus on gender, I wondered how much of the continued racial unrest would overshadow their conversation. Topics for discussion were provided to the bishops beforehand; the list included identifying barriers that Black clergy women face in the search for church employment; and the stressors experienced by women clergy in balancing their roles at home with their roles in the Church. I also was interested in what they believed was needed to make meaningful and lasting changes for gender equality for women in the Church.

If there was time, I also wanted to know what they thought about the invitation from Presiding Bishop Michael B. Curry and President of the House of Deputies the Rev. Gay Clark Jennings to all Episcopalians to participate in a survey about sexual misconduct in the denomination to assist the work of the Task Force on Women, Truth, and Reconciliation.[2] This was one of several task forces that had been working on sexual harassment, exploitation, and abuse.

Given that this October session with the five bishops was to focus on gender, I recognized that it had been only forty-five years ago that women were first ordained as priests in the Episcopal Church. Before beginning our meeting, I recalled earlier conversations with the bishops about what it was like to be a woman and aspire to ordination today.

Bp Jennifer: There were always women at the altar at the Episcopal churches I attended. I didn't know that women couldn't always be ordained for the longest time because that's all I ever saw in the churches I happened to stumble into. And when I went to college, there was a woman associate on staff at the Episcopal church on my campus. I didn't think much about race or women and things until I graduated.

After I moved back to New York City, I started going to Trinity Church Wall Street, which is where I was originally baptized and, again, an integrated congregation. Women were everywhere and there were Black clergy on staff. I think they had like four Black priests on the staff at the time, so I am thinking that this is the church. Except Trinity is like no place else and I didn't kind of get that for a while.

I was invited to discern ordination by a female priest at Trinity and there was never an issue of having to fight for opportunities to serve. It was just like, "Of course you can serve. Do whatever like you dream of." So, it just makes me think about how often those opportunities are withheld today from all kinds of people.

Bp Kym: I remember at the AME church when we had our first seminarian intern that was a woman. This was in 1983 and it was scandalous that the pastor was going to let a woman be in that role. I just remember thinking, *Why not?* I do think that was sort of the beginnings of the stirrings of my own call to begin to question the role of women in church. Why can't this woman lead the church?

Bp Phoebe: When I was a girl in the '70s, women didn't play much of a leadership role in either the Baptist or the Episcopal churches. Women were just starting to be on the vestry in the Episcopal Church, but certainly none of the deacons or trustees were women in the Missionary Baptist Church. The most that a woman could do was to be the head usher or read the announcements and the greeting cards from a music stand on the floor. There was never a woman on the podium, never a woman preacher, never a woman leading pray. And in the adult class, if it was all women and even one man walked in the door, the man had to teach because of course the Bible said that women cannot teach men. So, I didn't really grow up with women in real leadership roles in either church. What got me to stay in the Episcopal Church was women's ordination because, like you, Kym, I asked a lot of questions when women finally could be ordained. But Episcopal Church was very racially segregated, so I certainly knew that I was Black the whole time.

Bp Carlye: About five years after I was ordained, my priest from my home parish found me. He was a white priest in a Black church, obviously. All the priests I knew in the Episcopal Church and in Roman Catholic schools were white men. I saw no ordained women ever, not until I was in my forties. When the priest of my childhood found me, he said he was beside himself about my ordination. He felt that if I had been a boy I would have been ordained sooner. There was a process for encouraging teen boys into the priesthood. When he looked back over all of his ministry, I was the child who had priest written across my forehead from the minute I walked in the door. That's who I was.

The good news for me was that I did not feel a loss. I loved the church. I loved what I was doing in church. I had no vision or picture of myself as a priest until a friend in the church suggested it. The role of church community was a key part of my discernment.

I also recalled an earlier conversation that the bishops had about their own experiences of being one of the first Black women to be ordained in their dioceses, and how at times, it was difficult and lonely.

Bp Kym: I ended up being sponsored by this tiny little mission in North Carolina where there were only four people of color in the church. There was one Black woman, an Asian couple, and me. That was it. And I thought, *Oh, my God. These people are never going to sponsor me for ordination.* Father Bob said to them, "You know, it's going to be rough because she's the first Black woman to go for ordination to the priesthood in this diocese." This was in the '90s in North Carolina. And this little church said, "Oh, we definitely think she's called. We'll do it."

Bp Phoebe: I'm the first Black woman ordained out of Louisiana and that happened in 2008.

Bp Shannon: When I was ordained there had been only one Black woman ordained out of the Diocese of Michigan [the Rev. Monique Ellison]. And when I was ordained in 2005, Rev. Joyce Matthews also was ordained; so then there were two more of us. The next Black woman ordained out of the Diocese of Michigan was only in the last couple years.

Bp Jennifer: There was a time that we used to keep the number of where you are in the ordination for Black women. After the first hundred, people stopped counting. And I think that's an important part of the story because we think that there's a ubiquity about Black women's presence that helps us to forget that it's not the case.

Bp Shannon: As I began having more interactions within the Diocese of Michigan and the leadership in the diocese, I started to realize that our church has some growing edges when it comes to women, but particularly Black women. That realization led me to my doctoral dissertation topic, and made me begin to ask myself, *Why am I here?* This didn't happen by mistake and there is something about me being a Black woman that is necessary for the Church. And if it is, I wonder if I'm the only one feeling like this? I wonder what is it that we have in common as Black women priests that has brought us to this Church at this time? I'm convinced that because as Black women, we understand the ways of creating community and affirmation, we help the Church become the Church that it wants to be. What I believe will help the Church I see right now on this [computer] screen.

The Discussion Begins

Perhaps because this was to be our last session together, I felt a need to bookend our time together in prayer. Bishop Phoebe offered the opening prayer.

We thank you, God, for this gift of another day of life, for the privilege of serving your Church in the midst of the many demands and stresses and pressures of our lives, both personally and professionally. We're just thankful for a brief opportunity to gather together as sisters to reflect on our journey and the ways

in which we can continue to support one another in this call. So,
send your Holy Spirit to be present with us this day as we enter
into conversation. These things we pray in Christ's name. Amen.

Bp Shannon: I experienced in seminary a lot of racism that I did
not expect. Saying something about it back then would have
created a conflict. People expected you to go along to get
along. It was really nasty, the things that people would say to
each other, thinking they were doing it privately. Once, I was
in the computer lab and I witnessed a conversation about an
issue. I thought how I needed to pray for the Church; and I
was afraid for Black congregations that might be stuck with a
priest that doesn't respect them.

I was pregnant during the last part of seminary. There was
another Black woman seminarian and we were constantly
confused with one another. She was six inches shorter than
me and she wasn't pregnant. You know, I was just a Black
woman. No identity beyond that.

Bp Phoebe: People called me Carlye when I first got to VTS
[Virginia Theological Seminary].

Bp Kym: I was the first female of any sort of African descent to
go through the process for ordination to the priesthood in the
Diocese of North Carolina. It was a big snafu from the very
beginning because I was already in seminary and I got grilled
a lot on why I didn't choose to go to General [General Theological Seminary]. I said because General doesn't look like my
church. I grew up in a Black church and I looked around and
there were no Black professors at General. I went to college at
Wake Forest, which is not a bastion of liberalism, but we had

Black teachers. So, I chose to go to Union [Union Theological Seminary] because it was important to me to have people who look like me teaching me.

Clearly, while I thought the discussion would be centered more around what it means to be woman clergy in the Episcopal Church, for this band of sisterhood, gender could not be discussed separated from race. They are Black women and that is their life experience.

Bp Jennifer: Sometimes when I would visit other churches as a guest preacher, I would ask if they would ever call me to be their rector. And everybody would nod their heads. I thought to myself, *You never had a Black woman, so the proof is in the living.* But if there were barriers or blocks, they were low. I applied for jobs where I didn't even get past an interview. And I was okay about it; it was not the call.

I'd never been a part of a Black church except to worship in the pews at St. Augustine's in Oakland in my last year of seminary. So, my fantasy had always been about a church that was integrated. And there were only a handful of them in the Episcopal Church that are truly integrated. I said "no" to some opportunities until I finally said "yes" and accepted a position as a half-time rector [at Grace Episcopal Church] and a half-time campus minister at Syracuse University.

The thing that I think made it so hard was trying to navigate the difference between race and class and the expectations around being a Black woman from a different kind of race and class than those attending the church. I was not the first woman rector, but I was the first Black woman rector. And I was not Black the way the Black folks thought I should be. I just was not fitting in the boxes and that was a problem for me really relating to people.

Bp Shannon: There should not be a ladder in the Church to advancing, some expected progression of things that you do. For Black clergy, and especially for Black women, generally you serve in Black congregations or with racially mixed congregations. But some places just don't have that diversity, so then where do you serve? And people don't necessarily think you belong in places unless there's Black people or a mixture. It was hard. I'll just say that. It was hard.

Bp Kym: After I was ordained, I could not find a job in the Diocese of North Carolina. The historically Black churches would not consider a woman. I interviewed for a job in one city and I loved it. I thought it was a great church and it would be a cool fit. But then I asked where I would live, and nobody could answer that question. Me and my white husband, where would we live? And so, there was no job for me in North Carolina. That's how I ended up in Washington, DC, the first time.

Bp Carlye: The minute I entered the ordination process, I became an African American woman. That is the first way people describe me. I heard someone else describing me as the African American woman who's in the process in New York. I thought, *Oh, I wonder who they're talking about,* thinking it was somebody I didn't know. Then I realized that they were talking about me.

Sometimes our church manages to be an equal opportunity offender. So, folks who are not white are then ministered to as a separate group. There's a tendency still to this day to think that way. We ordain Latino people to be in Latino ministry. We ordain Black people to be in Black churches. We ordain Asian people to be in Asian churches. Although we say that's not what we do, on some level that is what we do.

I also recognize this sort of separation by skin color or ethnicity happens quite naturally in a predominantly white organization and shows up in multiple ways. It took me a while to understand that my thinking may not appeal to the whole church. It doesn't mean it's not important and it doesn't mean it couldn't make a difference. It means I see like a Black woman. I don't see like a white man or a white woman. I'm not trying to see like anybody else. So, I just carry on because what else am I going to do? This is the life that I'm in. And I feel that every time we show up, somebody learns something not just about us, they also learn something about themselves.

Bp Phoebe: To Carlye's point, I wonder was there something about my embodied work in the Diocese of Louisiana for three years after ordination as well as in my first call that screwed it up for other sisters? Trinity New Orleans Episcopal Church had never had a priest of color. St. Philips [Episcopal Church] Richmond had never had a woman. This diocese [West Tennessee] had never had a person of color or a woman as bishop. I think the journey that we're on isn't about wanting to be the first. For me, it was trying to live into the call that God was asking of me.

As a Black woman, some of the bishops found that serving in a Black church was challenging. Managing generational differences within congregations also proved to be challenging.

Bp Kym: I was asked to consider being a priest-in-charge for a historically Black church. When I asked the bishop if they were going to accept a woman, he said, "We'll see." I ended up staying there almost eight years and it was a really hard slog every step of the way. For me, it was more about accepting me as a woman rector. I think there was some racism in that I was married to a white man and nobody was happy about that. But there was just so much in terms of accepting my authority as a woman rector, and it was just a really hard.

Bp Jennifer: I served at a parish that was half Black and half white as the first Black woman rector. I would always think, *If I was a white guy, how would this go? If I was a white woman, how would this go? If I was a Black man, how would this go?* That particular church had history with all of those types of people, but I had to be that first. And being a first was really hard.

Yet, I really felt called to be there, and I had to figure out how to relate to older Black women who had different kinds of challenges than I would ever really know. And I needed to learn how to relate to white women who were proud to have a Black woman in leadership, yet I led differently than all of their expectations.

Age difference also at times can be challenging. There were older women in the parish who would bring their grandkids to church. But their children—who were my demographic peers—were nowhere to be found. And here I am in charge.

I also had to learn how to be with people who weren't sure they wanted me there. There was conflict and that was hard. But I continued to love all of them. It will be a thing that I carry with me always. It has formed how I interacted with other Black congregations. As bishop, I draw upon those past experiences all the time. What does it mean to move through conflict and to try to grow a congregation in the midst of it?

The bishops also shared the extra burden they felt to excel as a Black woman, to be the first or one of a few.

Bp Carlye: I am my greatest barrier. I have been raised to bring that extra 10 percent to everything. I have been told that there is no margin for error or failure. That the world is watching. That my mistakes don't just reflect on me, they reflect on people that came before me and on people that might potentially come after me. This responsibility that I have to live fully into life is, in part, a responsibility to future generations. Someone kicked down doors so I could walk through them. My job is to kick down doors so someone can walk through after me.

There are times where that expectation is absolutely overwhelming and exhausting. It's an extraordinary burden sometimes. And there are times where it's something that just feels full of grace. I'm aware that I stand in the midst of a tradition that goes back hundreds of years, and I feel strong.

But it also is hard for me to say that I need help. It is hard for me to say "enough" or "uncle." I'm always going to tussle with whoever the opponent is to the bitter end. Sometimes you just need to walk away.

Bp Phoebe: To segue off of what Carlye has said, I also had a very similar family of origin narrative about the elusive goal of perfection. And when you read my bio, you know everything I've done has been a first. That isn't something that I'm proud of. I think there's a real cost—psychological, emotional, spiritual, and physical—to be the first to walk into a space.

In spite of all of the challenges, the bishops found Sundays to truly be their sanctuary and to be life-giving to carry on.

Bp Kym: I wouldn't have survived had it not been for two things. One, my bishop had my back at every turn. The other piece was that church on Sunday was like a little slice of heaven. I mean, I worshiped in that church. I didn't just lead worship. I worshiped in that church. That was my food and my nourishment and what sustained me. Sunday was the one day that was good all around.

Bp Shannon: It's funny, Kym, how you said that Sunday was always perfect. That was my experience too, one of the oldest Black churches in the Episcopal Church. Nobody expected that they would call a woman to be their rector. It was hell on some days or even for some weeks. But Sundays, I mean, we all lived for Sundays because it was amazing. I couldn't have done it without Sunday.

For those who were mothers, decisions about whether to pursue new opportunities weighed heavily on the bishops.

Bp Jennifer: It was 2015 and I was waiting for profiles to come out. In the meantime, there was all of this upheaval in the country because Mike Brown had been murdered and LaQuan

McDonald had been shot in Chicago.[3] All these Black men were being shot left and right. It was that summer before the bad summer of 2016 where there was just lots of agony and pain in being Black in this country.

And I was a mom thinking, "There's no way I can be bishop and be a mom at the same time the way I want to be a mom to a Black son."

Bp Kym: It became very clear to me that my three-year-old did not inhabit his gender the way his other brothers did, that he was somewhere on the queer spectrum. I wanted my son to be accepted and loved as a beloved child of God for who he was. If that meant he wanted to wear pink sneakers and a sparkle t-shirt, that was okay.

I always tell this story. It was a time when I was considering a new call in Washington, DC. I was there at St. Margaret's for the rummage sale, interviewing with the folks. My little boy wanders into the jewelry department and asks if they have any tiaras. The woman behind the booth said, "No, sweetie, but we have some wonderful beads. Would you like to try some?" Nobody batted an eye. I mean, here's my little boy with like ten beaded necklaces around his neck, walking around feeling fabulous. It was just such a testament to how that congregation inhabited and understood gender as a community. It was a good place for my kid to figure out himself.

I was recently on a call with over one hundred other women and they were talking about being a Black mother, and how to talk to their children. And I was really honest. I told them that I have two conversations with my children. With my daughter of fairer hue with green eyes and blond hair, I remind her that she must use the privilege afforded to her by people thinking she's white to be a disrupter. When they forget who you are, you must remind them. And to my oldest child, I tell him that when the police come up and you're with your best friend, you be his white shield for all that you can because that is a privilege you have and you have to pay that forward. To my twins who look like me, I've had to remind them that while there are threats in the world, I don't want them to live their life in fear.

I want my children to know that they are valuable, that they are precious, that they have worth. One of the things I tell my kids is that they have to learn that Black people have endured so much in this country. And we're not going to let anyone take our joy. We're just not.

As the only single woman among the five bishops, Bishop Phoebe shared an important perspective that I imagine other single women clergy experience.

Bp Phoebe: As a single woman, when I was an associate rector, I was expected to cover somebody else's duties because they were going to soccer practice or they needed to take a day off for a field trip with their child. When I would ask to leave early for an exercise class or things of that nature, the answer was often "no." So, I find that if you are single going through this vocation, there's the assumption that you will not only give more time but that you have more time. People with a spouse or partner or children get the benefit of the doubt; their request is legitimate. They get additional time above and beyond while single folks do not.

Other people might believe that you have no legitimate excuse; you don't really have a life, so cover for this person. At times, it's been a struggle for me to say, "My life is important. I am not a fraction. I am not a half or a third. One is a whole number." But the larger culture will certainly lead you to believe that a family of one isn't really a family. And because so many people in the church are married or partnered, you may not be aware of that aspect of what it's like to go through ordained ministry as a single, nonpartnered person.

The conversation moved to the final question: what do you believe is needed to make meaningful and lasting changes for Black women to be equal in the Church?

Bp Shannon: Embodiment. I mean, people have to realize that the Church isn't going to fall apart or die if led by a Black man or Black woman. I think prayer and commitment opens up that space for change.

Bp Carlye: I think we still have to do the hard nitty-gritty. We have to look at our own internal systems. We have to make changes, starting with recruitment. You cannot recruit people of color when they're in college. You have got to be all over them when they're seven years old because once they're in that college group, they're headed off to something else. They're not thinking about church.

It's also figuring out how to do bias blind interviewing as well as how to compensate in such a way that you can call people and keep them. In some dioceses, it's difficult to keep a person of color. They get in there, get their feet wet, and then they go someplace where they can afford to raise their families.

Bp Shannon: And calling it out. I mean sitting with the vestry and calling out when they hold a woman to a higher standard than for a man.

Bp Jennifer: Can I just say "yes" to all that? There's a whole bunch of grieving and loss that the Church has to do about the place of white men in society. We're all about "dismantle the patriarchy." But when it comes to the Church, we have to actually look at what that means for us as an institution. We have to see that we're really fighting white supremacy in the Church. It's not just in America. It's actually embedded and baked in the Church.

I've been watching the postmortems after the vice presidential debate last week [Vice President Michael R. Pence and Senator Kamala Harris] and so much of it was about Kamala Harris—her affect and her faces. I'm thinking that America is getting a master class in how a Black woman speaks on a national stage. We now all know what those looks mean.

I do think that other leaders such as Senator Harris are helping to normalize what it means to hold Black space and Black bodies, particularly as women. People come in all kinds of packages and we're not all the same.

Bp Kym: I think too that there needs to be encouragement to do that hard, internal work to battle with the imposter syndrome [unable to accept one's success] that is so real. One of the great gifts is to have people who support you, who see your gifts and encourage you in those gifts. I think that is so important.

Bp Phoebe: And to ask the question who is not at the table? It may be a Black body or a Brown body, but it also may be a really young body, or it might be a physically challenged body or a transgendered body. At every instance—whether it's been the white church or the Black church or at the diocesan level—somebody's not at the table; and there's so much fear associated with adding a seat or two.

Of course, there's a theological aspect to consider. Our God is a God of abundance and not of scarcity. We could add a few more seats at the table and we're going to be fine. I think that to bring down the level of fear is a real challenge for all of us in leadership. And maybe that's a special calling that God has given to the five of us in this particular era where it seems like fear is at an all-time high. How do we bring that sense of fear down?

Bp Shannon: A few weeks ago, I had a family situation with my brother; and so, I had to cancel a clergy meeting. When I was able to sort of get my head together a little bit, I was able to tell others in my diocese that Black people are getting arrested for no reason and being put in jail. This is happening to my family right now. So please understand why I don't have any more energy to spend on your pushing the envelope about COVID.

The work that we do to protect ourselves in relationship to COVID, well, that's work that my family and I do all the time, no matter what. My family has to worry about our physical safety every day. This is real. It's not TV. It's not a cause. It's not a hashtag. This is my family.

As bishops, I don't think that we're there to be a thorn in people's side, but it will cause some growing pains for the church. We're not there to fit in in a way that doesn't disturb what has been. It takes too much energy to fit a model that people want or that makes them feel comfortable. That's not why we were called.

Bp Jennifer: One of the things that the process has taught me every step of the way was the call to be constantly inviting others. And so, I think that this movement in the Episcopal Church to raise up women in general and Black women in particular has been about our understanding that this is the way the Spirit has worked for white men for a really long time.

For the sake of the Church, we all must be really intentional saying to others that there are these gifts that the four other Black women bishops have, and that we need not shy away from these gifts. The other vocational piece that has been given to me is what others have given to me—which is to say that there is something in you. There is this call. You can do it even if you don't think you have that gift or if you think that it is not the right time. Believe what I am telling you. Believe that God's doing something there.

And so, the joy of having all of this to be happening right now—the book, the call, the elections—it's like, I'm good. There's not another thing in this church that I can want except for seeing how swiftly change will come. There's surely a lot more to do, but this is a bit of watershed that I'm just really grateful to be playing a part in it.

On October 5, 2020, the final slate of the nominees who would stand for election as the 13th bishop of the Diocese of Chicago had been released by the Standing Committee. All four candidates were people of color: two Black males, a woman of

Asian descent, and a Black woman—the Rev. Canon Paula E. Clark, canon to the ordinary and chief of staff, Diocese of Washington. I asked the five women if having a slate of people of color was a fluke or a sign of changes within the Church. Big smiles broke out across my computer screen, and it was evident that these five bishops were extremely pleased.

Bp Jennifer: I'm going to take a little credit for that slate, just a little bit. Chicago is a brutal place around racist segregation and class. But knowing the people who are on the Search Committee and on the Transition Committee, and the hard but important work of the diocese's Anti-Racism Commission, I'm like, oh, my God. I don't know how long it's going to last, but I'll take it for the moment. It's an amazing slate. [Prior to being bishop, Bishop Jennifer served on the executive staff of the Diocese of Chicago working closely with the Anti-Racism Commission there.]

Bp Kym: I don't know how many of those slates we can have like this before it becomes "too much." We have women everywhere winning elections and still it's said to be "too much" even though for two hundred years there hasn't been any women. I just have to say that the joy of seeing that slate was beyond. It is just beyond.

Bp Carlye: I feel like God is having a moment in the Episcopal Church. I think of all the little places where people have been praying faithfully and asking for a change in the Church— not sure if they were ever going to see it or if their prayers make a difference. Still, every week they got together and they prayed that something would change. And clearly, the Spirit is doing something.

As our session came to a close, I realized that the truth-telling shared by these faithful Black women bishops could be transformative for the Episcopal Church. I was saddened to think that it would be our last time together, for there was so much more that I wanted to learn from them. But that was before the presidential election on November 3, after which I knew that I needed to hear from the bishops one more time. Bishop Shannon led us in our closing prayer.

Gracious God, I thank you so much for the gift of the diversity that you have gifted us within the world and in the Church. Thank you in particular for the gift of our Blackness and of our womanhood and for all that we bring to ministry in your Church. I thank you for our stories, for the love that we have for you and for your people and for this institution. We pray that you would continue to be with us in the ways that you have been. Open our eyes and our hearts. Give us ever more courage to do whatever it is that you've called us to do. To lead boldly, to lead as ourselves, and to rely on each other. In Jesus' name, Amen.

THE RT. REV. DR. SHANNON MACVEAN-BROWN

Chapter 6

WE ARE THE CHURCH

Setting the Stage

The presidential election was held on November 3, and while it appeared that Vice President Joe Biden was the president-elect, votes were still being counted in several states (i.e., Arizona, Georgia, North Carolina, Pennsylvania, Nevada, and Wisconsin). By the date of our meeting, the Trump administration had filed fifteen lawsuits claiming election fraud and Pro-Trump rallies were beginning to occur across the country, many including armed protesters.

While I had thought that the October 13 session with the bishops had been the final one, I wondered if we might be able to have one more virtual meeting to discuss their thoughts on how to begin to heal the brokenness in our country. It seemed that the book would feel unfinished without including some conversation postelection. What were they thinking and how were they leading? I contacted the bishops on November 11 and they all immediately agreed; however the earliest they could meet with me was on December 3. While Bishop Kym would be on a prayer retreat the first week of December, she also agreed to joining the meeting.

Thirty days after the presidential election, on the day of our newly scheduled meeting, the United Kingdom had granted emergency authorization for the vaccine developed by Pfizer and BioNTech. In the United States, the Centers for Disease Control and Prevention (CDC) vaccine advisory group recommended that health care workers and nursing home residents to be the first to receive the vaccine once approved. In spite of these hopeful developments, the CDC reported the highest single-day total since April 21, the United States averaging 1.1 COVID-19 deaths per minute.[1]

The pandemic was beginning a new surge and the country was even more divided. Within the past month, each of the bishops had responded within her respective diocese. Two of the dioceses were hosting book groups. Bishop Jennifer was leading a diocesan book study of *Tightrope: Americans Reaching for Hope* by Nicholas D. Kristof and Sheryl WuDunn.[2] For the Episcopal Church of Vermont (Bishop Shannon), an antiracism discussion would be held in December and January using *A Scriptural, Ecclesiastical, and Historical View of Slavery* by John Henry Hopkins[3] and the viewing of the film *I Am Not Your Negro.*[4]

In the November issue of the *Colorado Episcopalian,* Bishop Kym's opening reflection acknowledged the "frustration and irritation in this time of COVID-19, that we are locked in this waiting time with no end in sight."[5] The theme for the convention for the Diocese of West Tennessee (Bishop Phoebe) held virtually on November 20 was "Longing for Joyful Presence."

On Dec. 2, Bishop Carlye in her weekly message asked, "How do we walk through Advent in the midst of pandemic and division?"[6]

Thinking back to the question that Bishop Jennifer had posed at our very first session in May, I wondered if we could begin to explore further the question of "who is *we?*" when we say "we are the Church." Inspired by the Episcopal Church's Civil Discourse Five Week Curriculum,[7] I posed two questions for the bishops to consider: how to begin to foster humane, decent, and respectful discourse and interchange across differences; and how can they—as bishops as well as the Church—help to bridge partisan divides and enlarge the sacred space for debate?

The Conversation Begins

As they began to reflect, the themes of love, healing, and hope were prevalent. I thought about Presiding Bishop Michael Curry's sermon on November 1 at the Holding on to Hope: A National Service for Healing and Wholeness when he reminded us all that "love for each other is a value on which our democracy depends."[8] The bishops steadfastly reaffirmed their courage to preach and live the gospel of Jesus in the midst of turmoil.

Bp Jennifer: The starting point for me always is about what kind of relationships do we want to have. The desire to have a relationship has got to be primary in hard conversations. The reparative work that we're called to do now must be predicated on an agreement that relationship is something we actually want. The struggle right now is that, in many cases, we're so polarized that we don't want relationships with people who don't want us living.

I wrestle with how do I talk about fierce conversations[9] and, at the same time, make myself available to the possibility for relationships with someone who I think is so opposed to my very existence. I think that's a lot of what the politics have come down to. So, I am trying to find different ways of coming together to engage in conversations. We're reading Nicholas Kristof because it's a helpful way to get to the real—which is what people tell me they're hungry for. If we're going to be building relationships, we have to have spaces where we can be real with each other about the things that matter most.

Bp Shannon: You know, Jennifer, that's where I am too. I think I am in a different place than I would have been if we hadn't lived through this pandemic. In some ways, I am actually grateful for the pandemic because it seems like the things that we have been providing—to keep people in the conversation who are not invested in my own life—I don't feel like providing right now. I don't even have the bandwidth to do it anymore because there's so many other things to do. There are times when I've decided I can't be with others because I just don't have any checks or filters.

For Advent, our diocese has been invited to learn *A Scriptural, Ecclesiastical, and Historical View of Slavery*, written by Bishop John Henry Hopkins, the first bishop of Vermont. Bishop Hopkins was also the presiding bishop when the Episcopal Church decided to stay together and to entertain conversations about why it's okay to buy people. At a time when people are buying things for presents, we are going to be talking about buying and selling people, and why that was justified by a leader in the Church.

I just feel that we have gotten to where we are as a nation because the Church still has work to do. Staying in those fierce conversations and being uncomfortable has not been something we have been willing to do. We've not been willing to actually get down to the root to help us heal.

How do we reconcile with people who want to cause us harm? It isn't as though something was just broken because it was never whole. I do not want to reconcile with people who question my and others' humanity. [For example], the recent news story of how they were going to negotiate about the votes in Wayne County.[10] I can't just say that it's okay to throw my parents' votes out because they're Black people and they don't count in this process.

The people who have carried the weight of those who will not get down to doing the real work have been the people who have been harmed the most. In some ways, it is better to insist on these difficult conversations out of love. Because I know that Jesus is big enough and has enough love to help us through all of this. If we are unwilling do this work, then I become worried about the world and the Church, because this is *our* work.

Bp Phoebe: I haven't said a lot publicly about the election results. I'm in a very purple context and Shelby County is a blue blip in a very red state. When I get outside of the Memphis metro area, I know that I have the full political spectrum in my pews. I did have some folks encouraging me to launch a major diocesan initiative on the issue of race—either using The Way of Love[11] or any of the curricula that the denomination has made available. But I have learned that to have open, honest, difficult conversations about any topic is really hard in this diocese right now.

So, I don't think that 2021 is going to be a specific focus on racial reconciliation in West Tennessee. I don't know if it's going to be a fierce conversation training, Jennifer, but I do need to get my people to have open, authentic conversations. Instead, I will focus on equipping all of us to be able to listen and hear a different perspective, and to put ourselves in another person's shoes. This is training that will help in all aspects of our lives—on our jobs, as parents, as spouses, and as Christians. Once we learn that, we can then move to specifically focus on race.

Bp Carlye: It really helped me to just sit for a minute and listen because I feel like I'm all over the map with this. All through COVID, I've been inviting people to bless where they are. Rather than saying, "Oh, I'm sorry I cried," let's just bless the tears. When you're frustrated, let's just bless the frustration. Let's bless the anger. Let's bless the outrage. Let's bless the conflict. And once we bless it, let's look for what God is trying to do in that with us.

There's been a lot of talk about healing and hope. I find that, for me, the word "healing" is waving a red flag in front of me for all the reasons named so far, but most especially after you have kicked the hell out of me, my family, and all that I hold dear. I remember watching the Truth and Reconciliation Commission in South Africa, and how there was an expectation to go straight to forgiveness and healing. It's a lofty goal.

I just think for the average person, we do remember and it takes some time to heal. And there's got to be some confession in there. I have been talking to people about the rite of Reconciliation [of a Penitent][12] saying that every single one of us has a confession that we need to be taking care of on a regular basis. No matter where you land on this, we need to confess because we've got things built up.

I just keep trying to bless that this is where we are and that this is conflict. I need to keep naming the conflict, and to keep naming the fact that this is not political ideology. I need to keep saying that this is really risky behavior that can hurt people, and that people are dying. It's just that simple. I try to stick to the naming and not the judgment. I try to stay as far away from political names and political parties as I can, and instead I try my best to stick to the facts of what it is we're dealing with.

Our folks have been chomping at the bit to get some work done, and have been going at it in different ways. There have been some challenges, but mostly people are wanting to go about the work that needs to be done. For me, it's been a matter of figuring out what are the effective ways to move along. I don't want to skim the surface. I want us to go down deep because I think we're at the end of a forty-four-year skimming of the surface when it comes to race. I think we thought we were done. We hit 1975 and we're like, "Woo hoo, done, finished." But clearly we're not done, not by a long stretch. So, I want to figure out how we go deeper and then how we can keep things moving along.

At this point, the conversation shifted dramatically to how the bishops—as Black women—personally felt about the division in the country and their sense of an increased risk to the lives of people of color.

Bp Phoebe: Carlye, the statement that you made about how putting people's lives in danger is not a political ideology is so true. What has become increasingly obvious to me over the past four years is that a certain segment of our country doesn't see me as a person. So, in their minds, they're not putting people's lives in danger.

Bp Shannon: Right.

Bp Carlye: Right.

Bp Phoebe: Why do we have children in cages? Why are there hundreds of children that our government says we don't know where these blessed children of God are? I think the average person would agree with your statement: "Putting people's lives—fully human people—in danger is wrong." But underneath that, I'm not seen as fully human.

Yet, God is calling all of us, not just those of us who are bishops, to be a part of the healing, reconciling work of helping to bring us together. And so, we are women who are lesser than. We are Black, which is lesser than. It's so interesting for us to be the people in the system with the least amount of power or agency being called to say, "How do we help resolve this?" And, yes, sometimes there is anger, quite frankly, on my part. The victims are being asked to work with the perpetrators to resolve it.

Bp Jennifer: And it would be fine if we were given the power to do it. I'll be happy to take that on, but give me all the power I need to actually execute it.

Bp Kym: I feel that reconciliation, at least in my mind and in my understanding, has to have some element of repentance to it. It has to have some element of people to say, "Yes, we have not seen you as fully human. Yes, we have not seen you as God's beloved," and repenting of that. I cannot swallow or stomach another whole thing where we brush all of the damage under the rug and pretend like it didn't happen.

One of the most powerful things I have read on my prayer retreat was from a womanist [Black feminist or feminist of color] Advent liturgist where she writes about the "Mammy syndrome"[racial caricature]. It was about how Black women are supposed to hold everything up and bear the burdens and be grateful to do it.

Bp Shannon: We're supposed to smile too, not just be grateful. We've always dealt with these false equivalents, as if some opinions are actually opinions and sometimes it's just evil thoughts.

I remember one time when I was about to go into a church service, and these Latino children asked me if they were going to take their mom away and what we were going to do about it? Some people already had been deported. I did not know what to tell those children. I spoke with the priest afterward and told him that this is a personification of evil. He said that I could not call it evil. I told him that I have to because I have a responsibility to call it evil on behalf of people who look like me—people whom I minister with and I'm a pastor to. They need me to say that this is evil and wrong.

Bp Phoebe: I've been using the writings of Archbishop Oscar Romero[13] this Advent. I think it's just reminding me to live in the way that God invites us and commands us to live. It's a cruciform life. And in this day and time, if they would be willing to kill a man behind the altar as he is breaking apart the bread, what are the possible consequences in our particular embodied form as women of African descent?

All of us probably have experienced certain aggressions because of our race and gender. What is the price of this vocation? Nobody wants to be a martyr. I think all of us want to live a long life. But in the increasingly violent nation that we find ourselves in: is there going to be a violent overthrow if the election doesn't turn out the way certain people think it should?

How do we support one another to speak and live the gospel of Christ knowing that there will be a backlash? There's going to be a repercussion when we do that.

It was as though all that the bishops had endured over the past months—balancing their roles as diocesan bishops while at the same time feeling the depths of their personal anguish, and yes, even fear—had broken open a vulnerability and authenticity that I had not experienced before. A layer had been stripped away and the true essence of these sisters was being revealed.

Bp Shannon: I found that I need to be really up-front about how I'm feeling. You all know about that one week when my brother was arrested unlawfully and released. He's out but still has something hanging over his head because they can. On that day, I couldn't even bishop anymore. You, my sisters, got me through that day and helped me to decide that I couldn't be with my people right then.

When I finally was ready to engage again, I told them to remember that they elected a Black woman to be their bishop. So, there will be times when I can't be with you. Or I'm going to say things—especially now—that are going to make you uncomfortable because I don't have the capacity to keep holding it. But if we're going to really be together, I have to be able to be myself. This is new territory for me and as it is for all of you, so it's going to be difficult. Understand I'm not trying to hurt you when I say things, but I feel like whatever relationship we have must be real relationships. I hated being that vulnerable in that moment, but they said, "We have your back."

Bp Jennifer: Shannon, I think that vulnerability is important because I think the stoicism, the "not feeling" affect teaches people that this is how you are to be in the world and in the Church. The price we're paying for being that way is that people don't know how to be real, or they'll find other places that are not preaching community. But to be that way is not edifying the body. So, trying to find ways to do that appropriately and to be authentically who you are or who I am in any given moment sometimes is letting a vulnerability show. I hope being able to be vulnerable provides the balance to the real authority posture I need to hold. And I hope that people can see that we can be a lot of different things in one body.

The only way we're going to be able to move through this is if we can be vulnerable with each other. I see that as a core piece of the leadership that's needed right now. I think I've espoused this theory before, but when I think about who gets elected, I think it's the ability to be vulnerable that makes all the difference. I think someone who is warm, accessible, vulnerable, and authoritative can help the Church be those things. And that's who's getting elected. It doesn't even matter whether they've had broad experience across the Church. If they're able to do that above all else, dioceses are saying that this is the kind of leadership we want to see. Part of what it means to be bishop now is to show what being a real authentic human being is because we don't have enough models of that kind of bishop anywhere in the world or in the Church.

Bp Shannon: I think that we'll actually move forward as a Church because we can bring our personal experiences of who we are as Black women to the conversation around reconciliation.

I know that we're not willing to negotiate on the value of our lives and of other people's lives for whom we are responsible. We're not going to negotiate on that; it means so much to us because we know how to live through adversity. There's also a certain determination and willingness to do what needs to be done, to say what needs to be said, and to stick with things in ways that others aren't invested in the same way. This is part of how the Church is becoming the Church we dream of.

Bp Kym: The other piece for me is how do you lead? I know you, my sisters, like me have seen so many clergy leading their churches like they're feudal lords in some fiefdom. For me, that's not what we're called to as leaders. When I talk about raising up lay leadership, some clergy seem to be so threatened because we are calling for a transformational way of our church being church.

As the time was drawing to an end, the bishops expressed their appreciation for one another during these past months of the double pandemic. This band of sisterhood, indeed, had formed a posse—a group of trusted girlfriends—to support one another.

Bp Carlye: It's helped me immensely to have all of you. God is so smart. I don't mean that to diminish God at all; and God doesn't need me to think God is smart, but God is so smart. What a smart thing to do to give us a posse. God bless you, Jennifer, for how long you were in it by yourself.

I look at like what we were dealing with when it all first started—with COVID and the racial killings. I was having such a hard time figuring out what to say. I was in a time delay lag. But when we talked, I realized it wasn't just me. It is all of us because this is hitting our own households.

I was being asked, "What do you think, bishop?" And I'm thinking that I am losing my mind here. I'm scared to death. There's a lot of Hughes—my extended family—who are walking around that I'm worried about. I need to know where they are. I need to know everyone is okay. I am unable to attend to anyone's spiritual needs until I know that my family is safe.

To hear that each of you were having your version of the same lag was a relief. It helped me to know that the delay or lag was normal and that I was going to be okay. We were all going to be okay, doing this in our own time. That helped me navigate this crazy dichotomy of wanting to serve the people for whom I have oversight but also to acknowledge that this hits me at home.

When I wept in the midst the clergy meeting at the beginning of COVID, we were talking about stopping in-person gatherings and worship. I knew I needed to rely on the clergy to take care of people who would want to gather no matter what. We talked about the challenges with the elderly and people of color. When I stopped speaking after I said African American, I had planned to say, "I trust you." I could not get the words out because I was afraid for our Black and Brown parishioners. I was not sure I trusted anyone with their care. I remained silent as my tears fell, trying to regain my composure. And then the clergy started saying, "We got you. Don't worry, bishop. We have this. You can trust us." As it turns out, they were right. The clergy of the diocese have risen to these months of challenge and I trust them.

Bp Phoebe: I had a joint meeting with the Standing Committee, the Bishop's Council, and my chancellors. We were talking about the issues that we are facing as a nation and how some of that is being manifested in the Church. There was something that was so obvious to me from our lens of being women of color, that the majority of the white people in the room were not getting. And I didn't know what to say or how to get them to understand how this is resonating with me. In hindsight, I said some things that I might have not said if I had not been emotional. I wasn't crying, but I just said, "This isn't a joke to me." In that moment, it was just the human being of Phoebe trying to say, "This is life and death. This is not a game."

The most important thing in my life is my relationship with Christ and my trying to be a disciple. But sometimes I don't know how to convey with the right tone or the right balance so that people really understand how much this pains me personally. I know that I need more tools in my tool kit on how to say what I feel without shaming or condemning. I find that the very stoic, measured, tempered response sometimes doesn't adequately express what it is we all have been feeling during this time.

Bp Carlye: I can't help but wonder, Phoebe, if that isn't the gift that God has given to your people through you? I mean, I think we inevitably measure ourselves by what we think is the appropriate way to handle things. But it's not by happenstance or mistake that we are where we are. We all know the Spirit put us here for a reason; and that which we are in right now seems to be part of that reason. So, maybe that is part of the deal. Maybe it was all of that kind of papering over of things—the let's make it nice, let's make it appropriate, let's make it no fuss, no muss—for so many years that has led us to where we are right now. Because everything about our system is falling apart.

Bp Jennifer: I do want to tie it back to Michael Curry too. Just listening to this most recent round of conversation, I am wondering if Michael Curry had not become presiding bishop in 2015, would my election have happened in 2017?

I believe that how we see who's leading and how they lead really, really matters. I am thinking about the progression of presiding bishops in the time I've been a part of the Episcopal Church, which would have been Browning, Griswold, Jefferts Schori, and now Michael Curry.[14] You can sort of see the progression in how the person and the personality provided the permission to be a little bit more open and authentic about who we are and how we're feeling. We don't have to be the "frozen chosen" that has been our brand.

When she became the first woman bishop, Barbara Harris was able to be authentically who she was as she broke a barrier for more than just her gender and her race. For a while, I think people just said, "Oh, that's Barbara." Like she can say or do whatever she wants to. So now, here we are, the daughters of her legacy, embodying it in our own way but holding it really, really differently than someone who's not a Black person would hold it.

I hope the Church is able to say, "Yes, this is who we are." And if the next presiding bishop is a white person or if the next bishop of Indianapolis is a white man, I hope that we've opened up something different for how we think Christian community can be and look like. But I think a lot of it goes back to how Michael Curry has made it possible for us.

Our time together had come to an end. Finally, I had the answer to the question "who is we?" Beginning with Bishop Barbara Harris and followed by Bishop Gayle Harris—and what I can only imagine were sexist and racist hurdles and barriers they had to navigate through their episcopacy—this band of sisterhood represents the transformative power of God working within the Church. There is a vision and a deep commitment for the Episcopal Church to become a welcoming place for authentic, vulnerable, inclusive, spirit-filled, truth-telling people who can join together to say, "We are the Church."

The power of God transforming the Church was evident nine days later, December 12, when the Diocese of Chicago elected the Rev. Canon Paula E. Clark to serve as their diocesan bishop, the first Black person and first woman to hold that position. I know Bishop-elect Paula is being welcomed into this band of sisterhood of Black women diocesan bishops as they continue to live into the call that God has placed in their hearts. Bishop Jennifer offered the closing prayer:

Holy gracious God, we give you thanks that you have given us this day, another opportunity to be all who you have called us to be, each one of us wonderfully and marvelously made. We pray that you would help us to grow into who you are calling us to be, blessing us, holding us through our mistakes, helping us to see that there's nothing that we can do wrong if we are living authentically and following you faithfully. We ask that you will continue to be with us in this time as we go about the work of tending your Church and leading and serving. We ask that you would keep us healthy and safe. Bless our country in this time of transition. Help us to find ways to continue to speak truth to power even as we hold some of that power to be able to help us envision the fullness of our humanity and to live it most thoroughly and faithfully in Christ. And it is in his name we pray. Amen.

THE RT. REV. JENNIFER BASKERVILLE-BURROWS

Afterword

The Setting

When this book was first proposed, there were five Black women bishops in the Episcopal Church. Shortly after our last meeting on December 3, 2020, a sixth bishop had joined: the Rt. Rev. Paula E. Clark was elected on December 12, becoming the first Black person and first woman to serve in the Diocese of Chicago upon her consecration. In the midst of her very busy schedule—closing out matters in the Diocese of Washington, packing up her house in Maryland, beginning orientation and consecration planning in the Diocese of Chicago—Bishop Paula without hesitation said "yes" to an invitation to join the conversation—albeit as it was concluding, at least in this format, sharing her thoughts on "race, faith, and the Church" as she steps into "this band of sisterhood."

The Conversation Continues

I join this band of sisterhood cognizant that upheaval and uncertainty in our community and in our nation are pivotal in my life and ministry. Similar to the other bishops, my own experience of growing up Black shaped my formation.

My first memories are of moving to southeast Washington, DC, at the age of three. We were the first Black family with children in the neighborhood, and I vividly remember being called "that N-word baby" as my mother pushed me in the stroller through the neighborhood. Our arrival quickly precipitated the departure of white families, as other Black families joined us in the neighborhood.

My parents and other young Black professionals tried unsuccessfully to integrate the local white Baptist Church. I remember my father scooping me off the pew during the senior pastor's sermon and walking out of the church with other white and Black families to form the "Fellowship of the Free" in the basement of St. Timothy's Episcopal Church. The Fellowship's Friday evening gatherings were our family routine, worshiping with diverse families around the celebration of communion with freshly baked bread and grape juice, unified as Christ's body. These gatherings embody the ideal of what the Church and our nation could and should be.

The Fellowship disbanded, but the Spirit guided my path ever forward. I entered National Cathedral School (NCS) in the seventh grade when the Episcopal Church was embroiled in debates over the ordination of women, and I received my call to the priesthood during a Cathedral chapel service where one of the four irregularly ordained women priests ordained on September 7, 1975, at St. Stephen and the Incarnation preached. Her passion in her sermon about the importance of women in leadership in the Church was very inspiring to me, and I felt God beckoning me to follow. I knew unequivocally I was called to be a priest, yet when I shared my calling with my mother, she told me she did not believe in women's ordination, so that was that.

After completing my undergraduate and graduate studies, I returned to DC to work in local government. Stress in the job deepened my relationship with God and I began serving as a eucharistic minister at St. Timothy's. I also took vows as a Daughter of the King (DOK) on January 22, 1995. Little did I know that ten years later, to the day, I would take vows as a priest. At a DOK service I read the scripture and a woman asked when I was ordained. I told her I was a laywoman, and she said, "Well, you should be a priest." My mother, overhearing, said, "Yes, she should be a priest," finally affirming my call. The Spirit was again moving me forward.

My mother died from brain cancer in 1999, which escalated my call to the priesthood. Life was short, the country was Y2K crazy, and I knew I needed to pursue my call. I was discerned to the priesthood and entered Virginia Theological Seminary in 2001.

As I journeyed with the five Black women bishops through the conversations included in this book as they talked together against the backdrop of the pandemic and the racial unrest, I reflected on three significant events in my life that influenced my own ministry. First, on September 11, 2001, as the country crumbled into grief and shock, we could smell the Pentagon from the campus of Virginia Theological Seminary. I knew our nation and my ministry would be forever impacted by that fateful day. Second, I became a member of the Diocese of Washington staff shortly after the exoneration of Trayvon Martin's murderer. With the country reawakening to the atrocities of racism, I set about trying to raise awareness and educate the diocese about the sins of racism and white supremacy. Third, early in the Chicago search process, the country shut down under the weight of COVID-19. Early in the pandemic, stricken by COVID-19 myself, I became a passionate preacher and activist on the dual pandemics of COVID and racism and their devastating effects on Brown, Black, and Indigenous people.

Like my sister bishops, Bishop Jennifer Baskerville-Burrows is a large influence in my life, for it is she who reached out and convinced me to apply in Chicago. I was ecstatic to be part of the historic slate with all people of color in the Diocese of Chicago and I did not care who was called—because I knew, no matter what, we all were qualified, and God would be glorified. I was humbled, anxious, and elated when elected, and now I am in the 2020 class of so-called "COVID bishops."

I am writing this a month after the storming of the Capitol by domestic terrorists. President Biden and Vice President Harris have taken their oaths of office, and poet Amanda Gorman has uttered prophetic words, capturing this time for us as Christians and Black women bishops. Gorman said, "For there is always light, if only we're brave enough to see it. If only we're brave enough to be it."

I am thankful to join this brave band of sisters who, beginning with Bishop Barbara Harris, see, bear, and embody the light of Christ, and I am grateful for all whom they inspire as my ministry begins in the Diocese of Chicago.

Gracious loving, and life-giving God, we thank you for the opportunity to serve you during this time of uncertainty, disorientation, and upheaval. The ravages of pandemic, rampant racism, and disunity focus our faith on You alone to heal our souls, our bodies, our nation, and the world. You exhort us repeatedly in scripture, "Do not be afraid." Grant us the blessing of being brave, as we seek to do your will in our ministry, in our dioceses, our communities, and our Church. May we see your light, bear your light, embody your light, and carry your light, as we humbly lead and exhort your people to spread the light and love of Jesus in the midst all whom we live, and move and have our being. AMEN.

PAULA E. CLARK

Notes

Introduction

1. The purpose of the Gathering of Leaders is to assist in the empowerment, support, and development of young, creative, proven clergy-leaders in the Episcopal Church.

2. The Rt. Rev. Catherine Elizabeth Maples Waynick was the 10th bishop of the Diocese of Indianapolis from 1997 to 2017.

3. Mary Frances Schjonberg, "Women Are Joining the House of Bishops at Unprecedented Rate," Episcopal News Service, July 1, 2019, https://www.episcopalnewsservice.org/2019/07/01/women-are-joining-the-house-of-bishops-at-unprecedented-rate/.

Chapter 1

1. Johns Hopkins Center for Health Security, June 1, 2020, Baltimore, MD.

2. The Rt. Rev. Phoebe A Roaf, "A Message from Bishop Phoebe," Diocese of West Tennessee, June 2, 2020, https://episwtn.org/a-message-from-bishop-phoebe-june-2-2020/.

3. The Rt. Rev. Mariann Edgar Budde, "Peaceful Protesters Tear Gassed to Clear Way for Trump Church Visit," interviewed by Steve Inskeep, NPR Morning Edition, June 2, 2020, https://www.npr.org/2020/06/02/867578108/peaceful-protesters-tear-gassed-to-clear-way-for-trump-church-visit.

4. The Rt. Rev. Dr. Shannon MacVean-Brown, "Reaffirming Our Renunciation of Evil," Diocese of Vermont, June 1, 2020,

https://diovermont.org/2020/06/02/reaffirming-our-renunciation
-of-evil-a-message-from-bishop-shannon/.

5. The Rt. Rev. Carlye J Hughes, "A Pastoral Letter from Bishop
Hughes: What Direction Shall We Choose as Health Crisis and
Racism Intersect with Faith and Politics?," Diocese of Newark, June
2, 2020, https://dioceseofnewark.org/content/pastoral-letter
-bishop-hughes-what-direction-shall-we-choose-health-crisis-and
-racism.

6. The Episcopal Church Office of Government Relations,
"The Episcopal Church's Response to Racist Violence," June 2, 2020,
https://www.episcopalchurch.org/ogr/the-episcopal-churchs
-response-to-racist-violence/.

7. The controversy of kneeling during the national anthem as
a sign of peaceful protest began in 2016 with the San Francisco
49ers quarterback Colin Kaepernick, and was highly politicized
as being unpatriotic. The death of George Floyd spurred athletes
to "take a knee" at major sports events. In June 2020, in support of
Black Lives Matter, protesters gathered at the Academy of Motion
Pictures Arts and Sciences. On August 26, 2020, the National
Basketball Association, the National Hockey League, and Major
League Baseball postponed games, as some teams joined the protest movement.

Chapter 2

1. Larry Buchanan, Quoctrung Bui, and Jugal K. Patel, "Black
Lives Matter May Be the Largest Movement in U.S. History," *The
New York Times*, July 3, 2020, https://www.nytimes.com/interactive/
2020/07/03/us/george-floyd-protests-crowd-size.html.

2. Johns Hopkins Center for Health Security, June 30, 2020,
Baltimore, MD.

3. The Rt. Rev. Jennifer Baskerville-Burrows, "Revised Diocesan
Reopening Guidelines," Episcopal Diocese of Indianapolis.
June 3, 2020, https://indydio.org/revised-diocesan-reopening
-guidelines/.

4. The Rt. Rev. Kimberly (Kym) Lucas, "Message from the Bishop: Season II Transition," The Diocese of Colorado, June 3, 2020, https://episcopalcolorado.org/wp-content/uploads/2020/06/TransitionII.pdf.

5. The Episcopal Diocese of Newark, "The Journey Forward: Guidelines for In-Person Worship in the Diocese of Newark," June 23, 2020, https://dioceseofnewark.org/sites/default/files/resources/Journey%20Forward%20Guidelines%202020.

6. Bishop Shannon's mother was a school principal and had established Messiah Learning Center, a school for the children of Messiah and their Detroit neighborhood.

7. Not being Black enough refers to how Black people can be criticized for being "culturally white" (i.e., physical features, educational opportunities).

8. The Rev. Canon Spann now serves at Christ Church, Grosse Pointe, Michigan, as assisting priest and director of the Christ Church Spirituality Center.

Chapter 3

1. John Lewis, "John Lewis: Together, You Can Redeem the Soul of Our Nation," The New York Times, July 30, 2020, https://www.nytimes.com/2020/07/30/opinion/john-lewis-civil-rights-america.html.

2. Johns Hopkins Center for Health Security, July 31, 2020, Baltimore, MD.

3. The Very Rt. Rev. Michael Curry, "Episcopal Church House of Bishops: Sermon from the Presiding Bishop," The Episcopal Church, July 29, 2020, https://www.episcopalchurch.org/public affairs/episcopal-church-house-of-bishops-sermon-from-the-presiding-bishop/.

4. The Rt. Rev. Mark Hollingsworth, "A Message from Bishop Hollingsworth," The Episcopal Diocese of Ohio, August 18, 2020, https://dohio.org/blog/may-2020/a-message-from-the-bishop-regarding-in-person-rega.

Chapter 4

1. The Rev. Dr. Shannon MacVean-Brown, "Womanist Theory: An Appreciative Agenda for the Episcopal Church" (PhD diss, Ecumenical Theological Seminary, 2014), 4.

2. Yasmeen Abutaleb and Josh Dawsey, "New Trump Pandemic Adviser Pushes Controversial 'Herd Immunity' Strategy, Worrying Public Health Officials," *The Washington Post*, August 31, 2020, https://www.washingtonpost.com/politics/trump-coronavirus-scott-atlas-herd-immunity/2020/08/30/925e68fe-e93b-11ea-970a-64c73a1c2392_story.html.

3. Mary Frances Schjonberg, "Women Are Joining the House of Bishops at Unprecedented Rate," *Episcopal News Service*, July 1, 2019, https://www.episcopalnewsservice.org/2019/07/01/women-are-joining-the-house-of-bishops-at-unprecedented-rate/. Since this article was published, the Rt. Rev. Deon Kevin Johnson, a Black male, became the 11th bishop of the Episcopal Diocese of Missouri, and the Rt. Rev. Paula Clark, a Black female, became the 13th bishop of the Episcopal Diocese of Chicago.

4. At the 78th General Convention held June 28–30, 2015, in Salt Lake City, Utah, attendees wore purple scarves in support of increasing the number of women bishops.

5. The Rt. Rev. Chilton R. Knudsen served as the diocesan bishop for Maine from 1997 until her retirement in 2008.

6. Begun in 2007, Beautiful Authority is a gathering of female clergy for support and mentoring. The Rt. Rev. Mary Gray-Reeves (the third bishop of the Diocese of El Camino Real) was instrumental in creating this conference and continues to provide leadership for this initiative.

7. Leading Women hosts a conference to bring together ordained women to learn more about executive-level vocations in the Church. The Rev. Helen Svoboda-Barber is executive director of Women Embodying Executive Leadership (WEEL), a cohort model for leadership development.

8. "Lifting as We Climb" was the motto of the National Council of Negro Women, founded by Mary McLeod Bethune in 1935.

Chapter 5

1. Johns Hopkins Center for Health Security, October 14, 2020, Baltimore, MD.

2. The Episcopal Church, "A Letter to Episcopalians from Presiding Bishop Michael B. Curry and President of the House of Deputies the Rev. Gay Clark Jennings," The Public Affairs Office, June 8, 2020, https://www.episcopalchurch.org/publicaffairs/the-following -letter-invites-everyone-in-the-episcopal-church-to-participate-in -a-survey-about-sexual-misconduct-in-the-denomination/.

3. On August 9, 2014, Michael Brown Jr.—an unarmed Black teenager—was fatally shot by a white Ferguson, Missouri, police officer. The phrase "Hands Up, Don't Shoot" became a phrase used by Black Lives Matter. On October 20, 2014, seventeen-year old LaQuan McDonald was fatally shot by a Chicago police officer.

Chapter 6

1. Johns Hopkins Center for Health Security, December 3, 2020, Baltimore, MD.

2. Nicholas D. Kristof and Sheryl WuDunn, *Tightrope: Americans Reaching for Hope* (New York: Knopf Doubleday Publishing Group, 2020).

3. John Henry Hopkins (1792–1868), *A Scriptural, Ecclesiastical, and Historical View of Slavery: From the Days of the Patriarch Abraham, to the Nineteenth Century. Addressed to the Right Rev. Alonzo Potter of Pennsylvania* (Ann Arbor: Scholarly Publishing Office, University of Michigan, 2006).

4. *I Am Not Your Negro* is a 2016 documentary by Director Raoul Peck, based on the writings of James Baldwin from his unfinished novel *This House*.

5. The Rt. Rev. Kimbery (Kym) Lucas, "Waiting," *Colorado Episcopalian* 82, no. 4 (Advent Issue 2020), https://issuu.com/

theepiscopalchurchincolorado/docs/episcopalian_advent2020
?fbclid=IwAR3M53f7zNLG4yVe4_2hC5o8z2WJFJlqEP0PJt1Cfy
ErcNNDl4EJTpuFDOw.

6. The Rt. Rev. Carlye J. Hughes, "A Different Way to Walk
through Advent," The Episcopal Diocese of Newark, December 2,
2020, https://dioceseofnewark.org/bishops-vlog/different-way
-walk-through-advent.

7. The Domestic and Foreign Missionary Society of the Prot-
estant Episcopal Church in the United States of America, "Civil
Discourse Five Week Curriculum," Office of Government Relations
of The Episcopal Church, 2018, Washington, DC.

8. The text and video of the sermon by The Presiding Bishop
Michael Curry from Holding on to Hope: A National Service for
Healing and Wholeness at the National Cathedral was prerecorded
and shown on November 1, 2020; and is provided by *Episcopal
News Service*: https://www.episcopalnewsservice.org/pressreleases/
presiding-bishop-michael-currys-sermon-from-holding-on-to
-hope-a-national-service-for-healing-and-wholeness/.

9. Fierce, Inc. offers training on how to have more productive
conversations. The Nicholas Center, a ministry of the Diocese of
Chicago, is an accredited provider of Fierce, Inc. and has provided
trainings for many parishes and dioceses.

10. In Michigan, representatives of the Republican Party
brought several petitions to the Wayne County Circuit Court
to block the certification of Wayne County ballots. This county
includes Detroit, Michigan, a predominantly Black city. These
suits were either dismissed or withdrawn.

11. In partnership with Forward Movement, the Episcopal
Church has developed a framework with practices and materials
to "The Way of Love: Practices for Jesus-Centered Life."

12. Reconciliation of a Penitent in *The Book of Common Prayer*
(New York: Church Publishing, 1979), 861.

13. Oscar Romero, an archbishop of San Salvador in the Catholic Church, was assassinated on March 24, 1980, while celebrating

mass in the chapel of the Hospital of the Divine; and is recognized as a holy martyr.

14. In the Episcopal Church, a presiding bishop is elected to serve a single nine-year term. Since 1998, the presiding bishops are: the Rt. Rev. Frank T. Griswold (served as presiding bishop 1998–2006); the Rt. Rev. Katharine Jefferts Schori (served as presiding bishop 2006–2015); and the Rt. Rev. Michael B. Curry (began serving in 2015).